1950

06/05

# Stillmeadow Seasons

# Stillmeadow Seasons

*by GLADYS TABER*

*Illustrated by Edward Shenton*

MACRAE SMITH COMPANY
*Philadelphia*

*To* EDWARD SHENTON

The Way to Stillmeadow

## STILLMEADOW SEASONS

From my desk I can look out through the old bubbly glass panes in the window. There are twelve panes above, eight panes below, and it is very hard to wash clear to the corners of them. But since the house was built around 1690, I can only be thankful that the old windows were never ripped out.

I look out past the great sugar maples that overshadow the little house, and on to the meadow and the hill where we planted the Christmas trees. The bottom of the meadow is a wild tangled thicket, half swampy, and there grow the wild cranberries and the dark wild iris and at the edge the wild red grapes with their sweet musky flavor.

Pheasants flash up from the meadow, and rabbits and woodchucks live there, and little velvet field mice, and now and then a secret otter follows the course of the hidden brook. The deer do not venture so near the house, but sometimes a red fox streaks up the hill.

We have lived here more than fifteen years, but a lifetime is too short to experience fully the beauty of the meadow, for every day it has new loveliness, new wonder to discover.

And yet it has not changed much, although I can mark how the young thicket has grown. We have left it to its natural existence and that is why, perhaps, it symbolizes to me the security we seek in a world highly unstable and changing.

The rest of our forty acres more or less has, indeed, been a little changed. The old orchard lost a few trees during the hurricane of '38, and thirteen came down in the back yard. The woodland has more fallen limbs, and the cliffs are overgrown. The baby fruit trees in the flowering lane are large and sturdy and have flowers in spring, and once we had two Seckel pears and three sweet apples! The plum tree did begin to bear just as it got some kind of disease and had to be cut and burned.

During the war, we turned over all the arable land to our neighbor, friend, and mainstay, George, and cabbages and corn and tomatoes and potatoes and cucumbers and squash grow thriftily where the Indian paintbrush and black-eyed Susans and daisies and violets and wild strawberries spread their delicate beauty.

Finally we began the farm pond. This, in a way, is a restoration, for there was a pond there once where the brook runs along the lowland, but the brook had been choked and lost itself in a swamp. When the great steam shovel was lifting the black loam up and making a steep hill of it, George stood looking thoughtfully at it. "That's

Stillmeadow was Built in 1690

all the land from my upper fields," he said. And it is.

The pond is eight feet deep, provides swimming in summer, skating in winter, fire protection all year round, and a place for fish to grow. The banks, set with wildlife planting, help birds through the cold seasons.

In our part of the country, nobody is ever quite sure where the boundaries of the land are. Old fences, long since gone, or gray rocks, or a certain dead chestnut tree, or a brook which may have changed its course, these mark the edge of one's property. Now and then a surveyor may scramble around a day or so and deliver an expensive piece of paper, but the farm folk go right on using the woodland or picking the grapes where they always have, and this is as it should be. We do not own the land, the land owns us. The survey we had when we wanted to turn over land to George for his house was like a Christmas present, for it turned out we had considerably more than forty acres, enough to let William, George's brother, have a house too.

Once in a while I try to picture what life in the country might have been if George and William had not lived right across the road, and then I know the main thing in buying an old house in the country is to settle near good neighbors. The natives in our valley are not the quaint folk so many writers talk about; the only quaint folk around here are the few city week-enders, and some of them are quaint enough for any fiction.

When we bought Stillmeadow, it was on a purely emotional basis. I knew the minute I set foot in it that this was the house I belonged to. I had no remotest idea of whether it was sound, and a good buy, and would be easy to live in. We never even looked in the well to see whether there was any water in it or not!

It was winter, and we had to walk down the road up to our knees in icy slush. There was the little white farmhouse under the great spread of the maples, and there was the worn doorsill deep with snow, and inside there was the great fireplace, blackened with the smoke of a century. Old iron kettles rosy with rust hung from the heavy crane.

Actually the house was in terrible shape. Renters had let the plumbing fixtures freeze, cracked bowls and burst faucets were upstairs and down, the wallpaper was stained, and the plaster fallen from some ceilings. The floors were patched with old cigarette tins. Debris sifted over every room; one wonders where all the old rags and broken bottles can come from!

There was a furnace, flaking with rust, and a cracked boiler, an ancient sink propped on unsteady legs, and rats had spread their ruin everywhere.

Climbing the steep stairs, we had to be careful not to fall through into the cellar.

We didn't have any money for repairs either. Taking on the mortgage was an act of rash courage; the down payment scraped the bottom of the barrel.

But the house spoke to me.

So we moved in and began to learn how to put on wall paper without having it fold back on us, how to patch plaster and not get duck soup from it, and various other skills.

Now, as I look back, I often think of all the people who lived and loved, were happy or sad, those who were born and those who died in this house. For there is a continuity of living if your house has sheltered its own down the long sweep of years.

In our turn, we have cherished it, warmed it, and it has offered us days rich with contentment. It has given us back-breaking hours of work and the satisfaction of tangible results from that work. It has given us fire on the hearth on long evenings, spring sunlight through the windows, cool moonlight on the doorsills in autumn.

This is a small house, but wide enough for fifteen cockers, two cats, an Irish setter, children growing up, friends who drop in overnight and stay three weeks.

The story of our life is written in white tulips set in the Quiet Garden, in tomatoes ripening on the vine, in puppies bouncing through the great snowdrifts. It is inscribed with the scent of dark purple lilacs, the satiny touch of eggplant, the swift falling of golden leaves.

As the seasons come to our gentle valley, Stillmeadow is always our personal adventure in happiness.

*I know a bank where the wild thyme blows,*
*Where oxlips and the nodding violet grows . . .*

William Shakespeare

## CHAPTER ONE

Nothing about country life moves one more than spring plowing. So much significance has it that I always stop whatever I am doing and just stand in the cool bright sun and watch and think, and my thoughts turn over and turn over and fall back in my mind as the shining plow turns over the dark, rich earth.

For plowing means the rebirth of the growing season; it means that Nature again will justify our faith in her rhythm, that we can count on this much in a world of incessant fluctuation. What would mankind do if spring ceased to come, if seeds ceased to grow, if fruit and flower ceased to ripen? No power of nations to destroy life would seem anything but trivial beside such a devastation. Nobody, in fact, would bother about the possession of atom bombs if those small dry seeds tucked in paper packets should all at once remain small dry seeds forever.

Well, there is security in nature, and it restores the heart to realize it all over again, as George turns the plow deftly to miss the asparagus bed, and the blade bites down again. There is thinking to do about the plow itself. I always seem to see, walking over our garden, the figure of the first man who plowed there, with a homemade wooden plow, homespun clothes, and his musket at the near end of the furrow, in case of trouble with the Indians. Smoke from the log cabin drifted blue against the blue sky, and how tall the

*The Garden is in the Same Place from Colonial Days*

woods must have been then! How deep the thicket, up the hill! I think of the labor of wresting the trees from the plot itself, by hand, with no dynamite to tear out the deep roots. I think of hand-turning the thick sod.

Now the plow that George uses would have been miracle enough for the first householder on Stillmeadow land. We ourselves have seen the change from horses to mechanized power, for George used to hitch up the two white horses for the plowing until a few years ago. And much as I admire the motor-driven plow, I miss the sight of the horses moving rhythmically along the furrows.

[ *18* ]

The garden has been in the same spot here for as long as anyone can remember. In New England, once you get a few tons of rock extricated from a piece of earth, you want to go on using it. You can get exercise enough taking out the rocks that have grown, apparently, during the winter.

Another thing that this plowing makes me think of is the plowing that goes on in one way or another all over the world. Being a simple person, I see the world as a nice round ball, and having no sense for maps, I can imagine the Burmese and the Chinese and the Africans all tilling their soil on rounded sides of the ball. But I feel a nice sense of brotherhood with all peoples who go out in the clear early morning and say, in whatever language they speak, "This is the day to plow!" There are small clearings in jungles where dark men go out to dig furrows in the black soil and plant strange fruits I never tasted, while the small dark women tend the fire and argue with the children, and purple and ivory birds cry in the branches.

I know nothing of these people and yet I know so much! I know how they feel at the day's end when the clean receptive earth is ready for the seed. I feel a kinship with them, though I am cooking corned beef and cabbage in the Dutch oven over the electric range while they are sitting down in the thick jungle night eating unknown food rolled in a green leaf.

I know how the women feel when the garden is ready for planting and the sleepy children are quiet and the man of the family has been fed. And if it be a place where the

women do the tilling, I still know how the family feels
with the tribal gods making this wonderful thing possible,
that food should grow out of the earth. Finally, as George
makes a last turn, I think how much we need to share the
food grown in this rich country. Nobody should be hungry
in all this world. It is the business of nations to distribute,
divide, feed the hungry. There should be no child in the
world going to bed at night whimpering because the simple benison of food has been denied him. There are many
things we cannot do—we cannot make all people rich, or
intelligent, or noble—but all people should be fed.

Dusk falls sweetly and softly in April. George goes home,
after a mere fourteen hours of nonunion labor. Up at dawn,
milk the cows, take the milk to the station, clean the barn,
feed the pigs, plow the upper fields, plow our garden. Cut
wood for the stoves. Repair the tractor. Get the cows in.
Milk. Work in the April night fixing the car. Roll into bed in
time to cool off the light bulbs before starting all over
again.

City people who move to the country to farm are often
a sorry lot, for they discover almost immediately that farm-
ing is not merely sitting under the apple trees of a summer
afternoon, but means endless work, rain or sun. On the
other hand, countryfolk have things that money cannot
buy in the city; the fresh smell of new-turned earth is one.

Sister Jill is already planning the garden, sorting seeds.
Early seeds can go in any day now: lettuce, radishes, those
nice crisp first things. Peas, too. In our valley you either
have early peas or no peas at all. They must mature in the

cool fresh days before the aphids rear their ugly heads and dry warm weather sets in.

Every year the seedsmen develop new varieties which are better and stronger than last year's, and it is fun to watch the vegetables improve. Some old varieties we like best, but new blight-resistant kinds are always added to our list. Last year 90 per cent of the tomatoes in our region developed a new and fatal blight, growing green fur before they ripened. This year we are experimenting with a tree tomato, and one tomato fills a salad plate—if it works!

We named her Maeve, for the great Irish queen Mr. Yeats wrote about in his poetry. An Irish setter, even at nine weeks, needs a royal name. Especially when Milson O'Boy is in her family. I had a dim memory of Maeve "with the bright and burnished hair" and also "with the lucky eyes and the high heart." And when we saw the puppies in a driving rain, twelve rapid-motion pictures, the color of Maeve's coat was like fire in the darkness.

We had decided that the cockers needed a big dog to be a companion, warder, and guard dog. And so, with my usual inconsistency, I chose Maeve, who is no fiercer than a baby pigeon. And when we got out of the car, her father and mother gave up chasing the hens and dashed over, waving wild flags of welcome, and at once embraced me warmly. Not in the manner of a watchdog at all!

At nine weeks, Maeve was just the size Little Sister and Linda had been when seven months. Linda was simply enchanted and hopped around, kissing the new bright one, wagging and leaping. Little Sister took a sniff or two, and went about her own business. Maeve sat quietly, obviously frightened, but with the grave dignity of her inheritance upon her.

In half a day the three were tearing the house to ribbons while the cockers taught her the etiquette of cocker ring-around-a-rosy and catch-as-catch-can and hide-me-find-me. Meanwhile, between removing the best sweater from them and saving the small rug, I hunted in vain for Yeats' "bright and burnished hair" and decided finally that I just made it up myself.

Now introducing a new puppy is easy, if you follow a few simple rules; but oh, how many people fail to follow them! First we got Maeve and the two sisters thoroughly fused into a trio. The next day we added Hildegarde, Melody, and Snow, and let them all have the yard all day. Finally the boys came out. If the whole crew had been thrown at her the first day, she might never have recovered from the shock.

Secondly, we let the cats look at her carefully from the top of the sofa. Maeve looked back solemnly for quite a while. Then Tigger, a Yankee Manx, got down and moved past with dignity. Esmé the Siamese jumped and flew. And that was over. The amazing thing, which shows how much more sense animals have than people, is that Esmé seemed to know right away that Maeve would not pounce like a cocker but would move more slowly and be more quiet. So she came up and sniffed Maeve and never even swelled her tail.

A new puppy should have its own bed right away and be shown it, and allowed to have it for its own possession. Maeve took one showing, and then got in and announced firmly to the other two that it was her own.

One thing some people never learn is that a new puppy needs rest. I have seen puppies made nervous, stop eating, develop difficult traits—all because they were never let alone to rest. They need quiet and plenty of sleep, just as human babies do. Being lugged around all day, squealed at, chased, having keys jiggled in their faces—all are bad.

Calling them incessantly is worse. A puppy never will learn to come to call if he or she is called all day long for nothing. We called Maeve only for food the first three days. The third day she knew her name and came instantly to call for any purpose.

Housebreaking is another hurdle, and failure to housebreak is nearly always the owner's fault. Maeve was a kennel puppy and had never seen the inside of a house. But we put her out regularly, letting nothing interfere, and the second night she did not even use her papers.

We also got her a box and put her toys in it. A puppy when teething will eat up chairs, rugs, bedspreads, anything and everything. But a couple of good clean bones, a sock stuffed with cellophane, a leather belt, an old glove which she can pick out and play with, help a great deal.

It was fascinating to see how different Maeve was, and yet how wonderfully she fitted with the cockers. She never hid or shivered when scared: she sat with paws together, head lifted, motionless. She seemed to be all legs, and yet when she slept she folded up neatly, cheek on paw. In play, she was not so quick as the sisters, but she lunged. And that tail—the only tail around, except Esmé's—was always waving. And when she saw the neighbor's hens outside the fence, instead of rushing and barking, she checked at once, lifted a paw, and pointed.

I do not actually feel a year older on my birthday, now coming up on the clock face of time. I only feel a sense of the value of the moments, hours, and days that are yet mine, and now and then a deep and passionate wish to do as well by them as is in me. Some people never have this feeling, but I had it even when I was a child. I can remember riding my old bicycle like mad in the early morning, with the spring wind blowing my braids and ruffling my middy collar, and thinking, "I must enjoy this, every bit of it." And batting tennis balls against the side of the house. The sun would be gold on the pale yellow clapboards, the grass of the lawn brilliant green, the sky feathered with a cloud or two, the good ping of balls on the racket, the swing of my arm—it was all something to experience as fully as possible.

Now, as time flows along, I sometimes think it is maddening how much one does miss—you can't ever squeeze the orange dry at any given moment. Something escapes and is lost. On a spring morning, who can see every brave spear of green in the garden where the daffodils will be established soon? Or every shade of delicate color in the heavenly blue of scilla? Or catch every vibration in the chilly melody of the peepers in the swamp? The music is cool and slender, and exciting; it is like moonlight and darkness together, it is the distillation of spring.

Spring this year is even more special after the storm and cold of the winter. We took a kind of arrogant pride in our winter this time. "It's twelve below today," we said. "It's even more of a blizzard than in '88." But having all the pipes frozen every few days, the doors snowed tight, the roads sheeted with glass gets to be tiresome before long. And I do not like night to snap down over day like a spring lid on a box. I like soft, long twilight with the sky glimmering until eight o'clock. Time to wander around the yard and watch the cockers and the cats, and still have supper before deep dark.

Maeve is still growing! It is amazing to see her with Linda and Little Sister, for they stay the same, compact little cockers, and she towers over them. They do everything together; they have just figured it out that Maeve is a cocker who got a little tall. Her Irish-setter red is near mahogany now, her coat as soft as fine silk. It is hard to realize that we have a dog who can open doors easily with one hand, pick my glasses off the middle of the table, and sort the papers on the desk, all without standing on tiptoe. She also likes to help George milk, so she gets me up in the morning to let her out, and vaults the fence we put up to keep the dogs inside. She flashes across the road and dives into the barn. George says she is a great help. Sometimes in the daytime she tries to get Linda and Little Sister over too.

Little Sister has become so much like our lost big Sister that we sometimes call her just Sister. Now I am beginning to feel almost stunned at the likeness, for George came in

*Across the Way is George's Family*

the other morning and said, "You know what Sister's doing now? She's covering her dish with paper before she eats!" Big Sister is the only dog we ever had who followed this etiquette. It was like unfolding her napkin. She always covered her dish with a layer of paper before she took it off and began eating. If there were no bits of paper available, she would use straw from the kennel, or fallen leaves. In the house, she could find paper napkins. And now Little Sister was laying paper on her dish before eating. George said, "She's Sister sure enough, come back."

Last year we turned the furnace off the last week in April. Some years we can do it earlier; sometimes May is the first possibility. Even when there was plenty of fuel, we used to turn it off the first moment possible. I like the house warmed by the great open fire in the stone fireplace, and by the little fire in my Franklin in the bedroom. And the comfortable old cookstove in the back kitchen heats both of the kitchens nicely. Upstairs you can run for your money, but who cares? It is fun to go to bed and watch the Franklin glow, and mine has little doors opening in two places so you can see the flames crackle, and the garnet embers.

It is strange how the habit of saving has become part of our lives. Maybe some people still waste, but I don't personally know a soul, either country dweller or city, who has not a strong conscience about any kind of waste.

At Stillmeadow we never throw away anything. Literally. Except used tin cans, which I always wish we could convert somehow to something.

Any clothing we don't wear constantly goes to England or a refugee collection. Books and shoes and materials go to Piney Woods School in the South. Here colored children get either academic or vocational training as well as food and housing.

Used curtains go to a friend in England, for she says the pride of a woman does suffer at hanging old sacking and frayed, mended rags at the windows. She has become a sort of curtain bureau for us and all our friends.

Then we raise all our vegetables and some small fruits,

and freeze or can or preserve every extra bit so that our house, at least, is no drain on national economy. For this we deserve no credit. Our canned carrots this winter were like plump tender slices of summer itself, and the store carrots at twenty cents were withered, rubbery, dry little things.

Every family with a yard can raise vegetables and live better, as well as help to make more food available for the rest of the world. The county or state agriculture department will test the soil so you can add what it lacks. And if you bury your garbage regularly, the soil will be enriched immeasurably. The Indians who planted fish in the maize hills really were smarter than they knew.

It pays to buy good seeds from a reliable firm. The germination on cheap bargain packets may be as much as 40 per cent less than with good seeds. And it pays to work the soil until it is fine and light in the hands.

Jill thinks it pays to plant earlier than the rules call for. But there is no use planting until the ground is warm enough for the seeds to germinate.

Here in New England, you may plant when the maples are in leaf. Lettuce and peas and chard go in when the maples are in bud. It is wonderful to look out and see the rosy mist against the soft sky and know the maples have given you a sign.

We also read the almanac. When it predicts cold weather, we wait for the planting. I love to read the almanac anyway, although I don't have any idea what things like *Moon perigee* can mean. It sounds nice. The almanac even tells you what are your lucky and unlucky days! Thursday is my lucky day—Monday is unlucky—and June and July are my months to be successful. On Thursday I am supposed to take the initiative in all things and on Monday, the almanac says darkly, do the opposite! Oh, me, I almost never feel like taking the initiative on Thursday.

This is the season of delectable dandelion greens. We dig them with a sharp knife, lifting the root and all. Washing them is a fearful nuisance, but a spray helps, and one wash in very hot water besides the cold washes. Cooked with salt pork or bacon, they are the most elegant of fare. Herb vinegar dresses them nicely for folk like Jill, but for me, I like them plain. They are best when they are young. We like the tenderest leaves raw in salads too. Digging is complicated by bouncing spaniels, but the dishpan does fill up nevertheless.

Daffodils, scilla, and grape hyacinths make spring inside the house. The grape hyacinths are my favorite, with their deep amethyst purple and pointed cones of flowerets. It is a little hard to raise them here, but in Virginia fields they grow wild, a cloth-of-purple cover.

April meals are casual. The outdoors is too exciting to miss. For besides the yard and garden, the brisk sunny days invite kennel cleaning, painting screens, settling the barbecue again for the summer, fixing the gate hinges, and a lot of other jobs. And on rainy days, which come often, the house cleaning goes on apace.

We go to town on the freezer supplies, for new vegetables begin with asparagus. Frozen strawberries for breakfast; *petits pois* with a mint leaf cooked in the pan, with broiled kidneys on toast, for lunch. Dandelion greens and buttered rosy beets for supper, with a broiler or a brace of veal chops. A compote of mixed frozen fruit is about the best spring dessert.

I am still trying to finish the reading I planned for those fictional long winter nights. One thing I have been reading about is world government. I do earnestly believe that if every American insisted that war be outlawed once and for all, if we stopped talking about the cold war and the next war, and if we organized into a vast body of opinion, other countries would follow.

The talk of increasing the Army and Navy and building more and bigger atomic bombs seems just as silly to me as if I built a grass fence around the barn and then set fire to the haymow. It is time to wake up to the fact that war is a luxury we cannot afford. The mass urge for self-destruction which swept us so recently ought to be overpowered at once by a mass urge for life.

How good the world is, except for this war mania that poisons the roots of being. So much love, so much compassion exists everywhere. Not a day in our lives but we see some evidence of man's real goodness, whether it be rescuing a stray kitten or sacrificing something dear for another. So much beauty too. Music and poetry and painting still create the shape of dreams.

There is the sky, now in April like a soft blue pearl,

and there is the moon, a silver shaving in her field of stars. And the air, breathing of violets.

In such a world, why should mankind turn away from the infinite richness it has inherited, and struggle to blow itself into black oblivion? I do not feel that we will.

When I get discouraged because the nation's leaders seem not to realize what the simple people know in their hearts—when, in short, they seem to have not a grain of common sense—I simply turn off the news commentators, and put the newspapers out in the kennel for the puppies' housebreaking.

And I go out with Honey and amble around the garden. Honey and I no longer race around or jump over things; we remember the days when we did, but now our birthdays come along, and together we walk thoughtfully. The dusk is violet-colored down by the brook.

Then Honey lifts her head and her dark dreamy eyes meet mine and her tail wags violently. A hopeful rabbit hops outside the picket fence, looking over the pea planting. Honey makes a wild dash for him, ears flying, nose quivering.

"I can run as fast as anybody when there is a real reason," she says.

My watch has been broken for a couple of months, and I have made a startling discovery with regard to time. I get along very well without being able to peer down at my wrist every few minutes. In fact, life moves along so easily that I have stopped going into the jeweler's and saying wistfully, "I don't suppose you could hurry a little?"

I have never known a jeweler who believed in hurry, certainly not my gentle old man. After all, he lives with clocks and watches going on like mad all around him; he can flick his tools and make a timepiece register any hour at all! So possibly he comes to feel that one day is as good as another.

At first, I fretted considerably. And finally a sneaking kind of freedom crept into my mind. I find it delightful to go to a tea party and just relax, visit comfortably, and never wonder whether I ought to be going home because look how late it is! I don't *know* whether it is late or not. And when an ice storm took down our wires so the electric clocks stabilized themselves at a quarter of nine for a day or two, I went happily ahead. We had lunch when we got hungry, and supper after dusk.

I found out that the washing does not have to be on the line at ten in the morning. And that it is rather nice to iron sometime late in the evening.

Of course I know if a man has to get to the office and the children must catch the school bus, it would not work to be so unmindful of time. But it occurred to me that many women might present themselves with an untimed day now and then and find just how restful it is to the hurried nerves.

I dare say eventually I shall have my watch back and begin dashing around on a split-minute schedule. But I do think it must have been pleasant in those days before clocks were invented and nobody ever knew exactly what time it was! For after all, sundials mark only the hours that shine!

The heart has its own time. How incredibly fleet are the happy hours, and how leaden slow the sad ones. The clock cannot hurry the sorrowful minutes a jot, nor clip the wings of the joyous ones!

Most of the April hours are happy ones—for even the dreariest rain means the quickening of the frosty old earth into a new splendor. It isn't just a rainy day, but it is a day to make the hyacinths grow, and lengthen the green lances of the tulips. We often have to put the furnace on, and snow sometimes sifts down over the greening lawn, but we know it is just a temporary note from winter and tomorrow will be warm again.

I admire women who can plan their menus a week ahead and prepare accordingly. I love to read a week's menus in the magazines. But my goodness, for our family it just would never work! We just wouldn't have the leftover meat from Sunday's roast to make Monday-night dinner. For somebody would get hungry late Sunday night, and poke around in the refrigerator, helped largely by Maeve and the cockers and Esmé the Siamese. A plate of roast-beef sandwiches with herb mustard and lettuce and a sliver of dill pickle makes a nice bedtime snack. And the cockers and the setter girl like all those bits that might make the stock for soup for Tuesday. Many and many a time I have gone briskly to the kitchen with a shepherd's pie or a baked hash and sour-cream dish in my mind, only

to find one leftover bone (earmarked for Melody) and one
piece of suet (the birds).

But I like to cook by emotions anyway. I like to make up
a meal from staples and a can of something. In winter we
make a game of eating for a week or so without shopping
at all. Then if we are out of rice, we use noodles. If the
bread is gone, we make corn muffins or spoon bread. We
pick out a package of meat at random from the freezer
and choose the vegetables that we have a surplus of, and
in the end we sit down to a very good meal.

If we find a package of ladyfingers on the shelf, I may
make icebox pudding for the next day and bake some date
*torte* because I found a box of dates behind the ladyfingers.

One reason cooking is so exciting is that there is always
something new you can make; actually, it can be a new
adventure every single day. We are currently experimenting with various things to serve with tea. Hot light tea-
cakes, coffee rings, little afternoon tea muffins—there are
dozens of them.

My mother and I used to have tea every afternoon when
I was growing up. At first I had cambric tea, but later I
grew up to a real cup. She used her mother's old silver
teapot, and I use it now, and when we sit down by the
apple-wood fire and pour the tea from that little fat teapot, my mother seems very close to me.

Mamma liked strong black tea. Last year we got one
of those tea taster's packages and tried to decide which
was really the best. And I confess I loved every one of
them. Earl Grey is very special, but so is Darjeeling. I like

smoky teas and jasmine-scented teas and every other kind.

The teapot must be boiling hot when the tea goes in. And the tea should steep four or five minutes. Thin slices of lemon pricked with cloves are all right; so is colored sugar. But for a family tea, we pour it out and drink it without anything in it. Just tea.

There's Still an Ox Team Down the Way

The hour to have your tea is that time in the afternoon when you feel blank. Around four, with us. Then you can attack the end-of-day chores feeling encouraged.

Recently in New York I went to a dinner in honor of several of the war authors. I was interested to see that the younger writers thought that war was the normal state of affairs, not abnormal, whereas the older authors felt war was abnormal and peace the normal way of living. Some of the youngest had never lived in days of peace at all!

When I came back from the dinner, I looked at my valley with new eyes. It hasn't changed much since the Revolution. A few more fields are tilled, a few woodlands have been lumbered, a few gas stations mushroom around the post offices in the little villages. There are road signs, too, and electric poles. But if you look down on the valley from the top of Sherman Hill, it is green and gentle and unchanged. The same white houses stand serene under the ancient maples, the same church spires rise to the same spring sky.

O beautiful land, I thought, surely you are worth saving! We have lived through the destruction of a large part of the world, and now let us have done with the blasting and killing and laying waste. Let us plant the gardens of the world again, reroof the little houses, purify the defiled altars.

The hills are tenderly green now, the unshuttered brooks mirror the hyacinth-blue skies, and the little singers in the swamp, the peepers, are making sweet music. The cockers race wildly after spring smells; their paws are deep with soft mud. The cats sit on the garden fence, their fur bright with sun.

Maeve is jumping back and forth over the picket fence, just because she can do it and the cockers can't. Her Irish-setter coat is the color of a copper teakettle, her plumed tail is a gay banner. Honey makes her way neatly along the terrace stones, so her paws, at least, will not be muddy. She reminds me of the Victorians with their parasols and lace mitts. The rest of them may make mud pies of themselves, says Honey, but she expects to come to tea and have her vanilla wafers in ladylike manner.

Wonderful is the spring! Full of wonder! And the sky so pure and soft, and all the sounds in the valley are the good sounds of peace. The sound of the plow turning over the rich earth with its shining blades. The sound of the ax cutting the firewood for the cool spring nights. The sound of the bucket creaking down into the fresh clear well.

And high over our green peaceful valley rides the triumphant sun, the sun of April, the sun of spring.

## CHAPTER TWO

May is a month for dreaming. The rich fulfillment of summer is not yet come, and the stern reality of winter is one with all time past. Winter, I think, has the frosty visage of a Puritan, and has no traffic with light-mindedness. And summer is like a Greek goddess, templed in green and robed in moon-silver, but she carries in her hand the dark secret seed of sorrow, for she forecasts beauty that must die.

But May is enchantment without shadow. May is the sweetness of love and the mystery of blossoming. And in May the faery folk come back to our New England hills from the lands beyond the sunset. For they like May too! My unicorn stamps his silver hoofs on the massed wild violets in the light of the May moon, and the glossy heart-shaped leaves bend as he passes. He crops the dark-purple and the blue-and-white violets, and his polished silver horn lifts the delicate rosy bells of the wild bush honeysuckle as he moves up the hill. To look on the fatal beauty of the unicorn is to die, according to the legends, but some folk look and live to tell of it, or how would we know what the unicorn looks like?

May is like lyric poetry, and is the time to read it, preferably aloud to someone you love. Poetry ought to be read aloud anyway, because the sound of the words is music. Like the music of Yeats:

"I will arise and go now, and go to Innisfree,
  And a small cabin build there, of clay and wattles made;
  Nine bean rows will I have there, a hive for the honey bee,
  And live alone in the bee-loud glade."

It is good for us, I think, to keep as much joy in life as we can. We busy ourselves with so many things that are not of the heart and spirit. We worry about money, we agonize over the terrible state of the world, we fret at household duties or business minutiae, we work, we argue, we squander our strength in a million ways.

And all the time the wonder of life is around us, the ecstasy of breathing air ravished by apple blossoms, of walking on fern-cool driftways, of listening to young leaves moving in the moonlight, and of seeing the twilight stars in the violet bowl of the sky. There is joy enough in one spring day to furnish forth the world, if we but knew it.

Even if life seems too difficult at times and grief gets too intimate with us and death raises his umbrella between us and the sun, there is still joy to be had in the immeasurable gifts of life, if we accept it. I do not mean to be a Pollyanna, for I always thought she was a tiresome person. But I think one should never lose awareness of all that is lovely.

The problem of suffering we shall always have with us.

When I read the figures of the casualties in our last war, or get a letter from a friend whose only son lies under a white cross in Switzerland, I know there are losses we cannot atone for. When my own mother died, there seemed to me to be no answer to anything. For a time the only universality was death.

And then I remember walking in the dusk along the quiet little street toward the house now so empty and meaningless. There was light enough from the sky to cast the lattice shadow of leaves on the walk. The sound of the river was steady and swift, and the air smelled of sulphur from the mills beyond it. As I looked up, a delicate petal of moon drifted into the tender blue, and all at once I thought, How beautiful God made the world! How wonderful that the stars still shine! And I was comforted.

Now in May, the cockers are in ecstasy too. Cool nights and coin-gold days are just their dish. And the good smell of rabbit fills the thickets. They never, never catch a rabbit, but they have prodigious games at it. And as I watch them, I know their merry disposition is authentic, for their tails almost wag off. A cocker may have sad eyes, but never a sad rear half.

Stillmeadow Jeremy celebrated his sixth birthday (weekly) by lugging a whole walnut across the room. It was a large walnut with a crinkled shell, and it looked as big as he did. Staggering with effort, falling over and starting over, he made his triumphant way. Then he dropped it, withdrew, and attacked fiercely. His growl is about as large as the sound of a small egg beater. He eats baby food, scraped beef, milk and egg, pablum, and has a dropperful of tomato juice and of cod-liver oil for tea.

Esmé and Tigger think very little of him, but if he lunges into their orbit they withdraw to a shelf and peer down. They seem to know he is a chewer and pouncer and lacks stability. Esmé shows her Siamese possessiveness by leaping on my lap and rubbing her head on my hand to indicate that the new little black thing is of no consequence.

Tigger, being a Yankee Manx, has a different idea. He is one of the most secure people we have ever known. Jealousy is not for him, nor doubt of our feelings about him. He does not yearn over us; he takes whatever loving he needs and then goes about his own affairs. He is never rushing up to say, "Do you still love me?" the way Esmé and the cockers do. He is a comfortable cat. We all admire his rugged individualism and so does Esmé.

I don't spend much time in May in the kitchen. Too much magic outdoors. But, we are always hungry in May. Jill works so hard in the garden that she comes in starving. If the children get home for a week end, they go straight to the kitchen to see what's available. Fortunately for us, Jill's son-in-law, Val, is definitely kitchen-minded. Happy the family that can achieve in-laws that seem indigenous to the household. We sometimes forget he hasn't always been here. He is gifted with a wonderful gaiety of spirit, an endless curiosity about how things are made, and a fine sensitivity to other people's feelings. And I think these traits should go at the top of the list on all those "What kind of man should I marry?" charts. Dorothy thinks so too.

Sunday my friend Maurice came over with a cranberry-glass pitcher for my collection. He saw it in a window in a junk shop, and popped in and secured it. It has little flowers painted on its rosy curve and the top is fluted delightfully.

With milk glass, a few pieces of cranberry glass are a perfect complement, and what nicer thing for a friend to do than to think of this while dashing down a busy street in the course of a day's work?

On thinking it over while scraping carrots for salad, I decided collections are valuable two ways: for the beauty intrinsic in the things themselves, and for the memory that is in them. Anyone who does not know the warm feeling of remembering the day a certain piece of glass or ironstone was secured has a real emptiness in his life. In my Wedgwood covered toddy cups lies a full glowing autumn day, a sky like a blowing sail, mountains like a symphony. And the ceaseless conversation of me and Bebe in the back seat of the car and the thoughtful murmur of Jill and my Cousin Rob up front. And the laughter of young Bobby.

This is all in the toddy cups, as well as the lovely old house where we found them and the extra delight of meeting some nice people around Elizabeth Curns' open fire. Even Bobby's trumpet is in there, playing *Sweet Sue,* and the tureen of homemade clam chowder that we had when we got home.

I like to go into the yard after supper, and sit a few moments and feel the moonlight slip into my soul. There is the house, steadfast against time, lighted and comfortable and

George and his Home

well filled with cockers and cats. There is Jill's garden, growing like mad to the left of me and there across the road comes George from milking, and I think what a fine thing it is to know George, with his strength and patience and thoughtfulness and his sunny smile.

And beyond my horizon, over the darkening hill where the old orchard dreams, are all those other places like Samarkand and Cathay and Alexandria and Tibet. The "old unquiet ocean" is rolling around the world and strange winds blow in the ship's rigging.

And here am I, and the May moon is weaving a silver web across the grass and the stars are young. And Honey is stepping softly to lay a velvet nose in my hand; Honey always follows my moods, so she is thinking too. Up the shadowy slopes moves my unicorn, making no sound with his silver hoofs, but the violet leaves are whispering.

On the warm, moon-clear May nights we like to sit out in the Quiet Garden. I call it a Quiet Garden, because it is filled with quiet old-fashioned flowers and herbs—a place to be tranquil in. In one corner, the old crooked apple tree is drifted with the white miracle of apple blossoms. The low white picket fence which encloses the small flagged area is half hidden by the young green of the rambler roses. The herbs are up; the lavender came through the bitter winter safely.

This is a spring garden, blue and white with accents of pale pink; it is small and simple as gardens go, the kind any woman could have on the smallest city lot. And how lovely it is. Tall ivory-white tulips, blue-lavender tulips, white narcissus, blue grape hyacinths, white and blue hyacinths, and white and lavender-purple iris bloom there in spring. There are the gray-blue violets called Confederate violets in Virginia. There are rosy cups of primroses, very early to blossom; and by the time the late iris is gone, the pink ramblers are coming.

The picket fence was supposed to protect the fragile stalks of tulips and narcissus from the dogs, but that was before we had Maeve. I don't know just how high she can jump, but I know it breaks all high-jump records. She clears anything around Stillmeadow in those long lovely leaps. We try to persuade her that Irish-setter red is beautiful against white tulips, but not mixed right in together.

We made the mistake of planting grass between the gray-rose flagstones when we began the Quiet Garden. Grass grows too fast, too thick, and mowing the stones is impossible. So we are gradually replacing the grass with lemon thyme, which smells good when you walk on it, and never, never needs mowing.

On these clear, still, spring nights the sound of the planes going over comes with sudden emphasis. When I look up, the plane seems to be like a ship sailing through stars. I imagine the people in every one that passes. There they go, travelers in the sky, bound for mysterious destinations. In their separate worlds they live and move and have their being, and when they go over this green valley, they do not even know that we exist.

This is a humbling thought. On our forty-acres-more-or-less we lead our intricate busy lives, and yet how small are our concerns viewed from the night sky above! Is it, then, so important to fret over window washing, furniture waxing, floor scrubbing? Or to worry over the weeds in the asparagus bed? We ought to spend more time, I think, opening our heart to the beauty of the world, especially in May. Just looking and feeling and smelling the brave sweet fragrances of spring.

Of them all, the lilac is the loveliest. There is enough beauty in a lilac for a lifetime. The shape of every tiny flower is delicate, and the whole cluster a pointed spear of exquisite loveliness. Then the leaves themselves are wonderful, polished and dark and smooth in texture. And then there is the dark, cool fragrance to enchant the senses.

We have amethyst, and blue, and deep winy purple, and white lilacs. The double and fancy lilacs are elegant, but the ordinary country-yard lilacs are my favorite. The white lilacs are more delicate in shape and odor, and white lilacs and white narcissus in a milk-glass lacy-edge bowl are near enough heaven for me any day.

In Northern Wisconsin we used to see them growing where houses once had stood, lifting their splendor by a blackened chimney or above fallen beams. Wherever an old cabin had been a home, lilacs remembered.

This is the month for planting, and as long as the world is so in need of food, Jill says she will raise everything that will grow in our rocky soil. She has mastered the art of running the garden tractor which we got last fall, and it is a wonderful affair, chopping weeds, pulverizing soil, tearing up turf. The first thing it did the day she got it was to plow up a whole row of our very best potatoes while Jill followed after it helplessly. Then it clipped through the gate and ripped up quite a row of the lawn. I was leaning out the window yelling, "Stop it! Stop it!" Which made Jill quite annoyed. She hadn't learned how to stop it.

Under control, it mushes along nicely and is the greatest aid for home growers we know of. It pays for itself in a short time in saving of labor hours and in better crop production. Mr. Hoxley, who helps in the summer, didn't think so much of it at first, but grew most devoted after it did a day's work in a couple of hours and left him time for a lot of odd jobs he had on his mind.

There is so much to do in May—and besides the garden, the kennels to paint over, dogs to wash, screens to get on. So now and then we leave it all, and go with our friends Faith and Frances for a long look at spring. Frances drives, and she is a natural explorer. She never takes the same road twice, and so we find lost country roads, hidden dreamy valleys, forgotten old houses. If a road looks impassable, that is for Frances, and we take it, coming out at the top of the world with fields and meadows below like a rolling wave of young green, with the scattered foam of flowering pear and apple marking the old orchards.

Frances always knows the best place to eat our lunch, where we can feast happily and look at a bank of violets at the same time.

Now that people cannot jump about Europe as they used to, and travel is so expensive, I would like to start a movement for travel in your own back yard. There is always something new around the corner of a country road, and it's fun to explore. Besides, says Frances, you can go home at night and sleep in a comfortable bed!

Some people might have said we had enough dogs, even before we added Maeve to the family. But now we have a new cocker too. His name is Champion Night Flyer, and he came when one of my dearest and oldest friends had to give up his kennel.

Flyer came by air from Oklahoma, arriving in Hartford at

night. When we drove up the next morning, he was ensconced in his case by the station radioman. He had been
fed, watered, exercised, played with, and the entire per-
sonnel at the field had become his bosom friends. He
wagged around saying good-by politely, then got in the car
and sat quietly while we drove the fifty miles home.

It was love at first sight. Flyer is a solid black, compact,
nobly built gentleman, eight years old. He has a fine sense of
humor, a nice imagination, and is thoughtful of everyone.
He was so polite, he never even took a drink of water until
he was invited to use the drinking bowl. He did not chase
Esmé. He let the cockers pile over him, and simply stood
waiting until they discovered he was acceptable. This was
most amazing, for our cockers are not usually decent to
visiting firemen.

He stayed quietly on the floor for several hours, observ-
ing. Then he said to himself, "In this house, boys *can* get on
the sofa," and he got up with a happy sigh and sat on the
sofa. In the night he got very homesick, and after I was in
bed two polite paws were placed on the edge of the bed, and
when I asked him up, he settled on the foot of the bed beside Honey and allowed he felt better.

He never slept there again. The second night he moved
to the sofa, making it clear that he did not expect the bed
except when suffering from grief.

He and Melody are the closest friends; they run shoulder
to shoulder all day, sleep together, eat from the same dish.
He is patient when Little Sister swings on his ear, but
doesn't think she is very charming. But he adores Melody.

They make a beautiful brace, we think, when they move across the yard together, dark muzzles lifted, eyes bright, ears flying.

The first time we left him at night, he greeted us on our return by rushing to the toy basket and selecting the bright red slipper and dashing up to lay it at my feet. I never had a nicer tribute. "Welcome home," he said, "I missed you!"

The only sad feature is that we did not know him for eight years of his life. But perhaps that is just as well, for I would certainly have broken a Commandment and coveted him.

"Oh, well," says Jill, with eleven dogs bounding around, "I like dogs!"

Living in an old pre-Revolutionary house is fun, but there are times when our modern ideas make things hard. Currently Jill is recovering from a bout with the stairs. I got the idea that we needed a good stair carpet. The stairs, like all those in houses of our period, are like an enclosed ladder bounding up sharply, and so narrow that you can brush the wall at either side. Long ago we fastened a ship's rope from Provincetown to the left wall, as a handy way to help mariners attain the upper deck.

The stairs were spattered, and had to be repainted every season. A carpet would be fine, I thought, and ordered enough. A set of metal rails came with it to fasten across the treads and hold the carpet in place. Also puffy cushions to go under the carpet.

Jill had an extra half hour the day it all came. She lugged

the roll to the top of the stairs, came down to get the hammer, and Esmé instantly went up to investigate, and with a whoosh Esmé and the carpet rolled magically down to the first floor. Esmé looked at the thing with surprise and made a few remarks in Siamese. Jill rolled up the carpet and lugged it back upstairs. She tacked the top down.

The rods were just the width of the treads, and the little hooks to slide them in went in nicely. The only catch was that once the two hooks were in, there was no way on earth to get the rods inside. Because of the walls! I suggested cup hooks instead of the closed screws, but Jill didn't cotton to the idea of cup hooks on the stairs.

On a modern open staircase, the rods simply are pushed outside the banister, slid in and there you are. But since the rods would not fold or bend, there was an absolute impasse. For two days Jill worked at the problem; meanwhile, the carpet rolled down every little while and nobody could go upstairs at all except Esmé.

"Well," said Jill, "if you don't mind my taking the house down, I can lay the carpet easily. I guess it's house or carpet; which do you really want?"

In the end, after a few trips to the village, she used finishing nails, drove them in, held the rods to the treads, bent the nails over afterward and finally got the thing stapled in place.

Since the puffs are pretty large for our small stairs, you rise to the upper floor in a series of feathery bounds, and it feels very lovely. And, defeated in the struggle, the old house has resigned herself to the modern foolishness.

In May we get all kinds of weather. We often have to put the furnace on, and the next day it will be humid and hot as fire. One day we eat in the garden where the narcissus is out, and the next we sit by the open fire and toast our toes.

But it is apple-blossom month. All over the greening hills and in the little valleys, the old apple trees are young with pink-and-white drifts of bloom. There may be something

*Spring Morning at Stillmeadow*

lovelier in the world somewhere, but I can't think what it would be. It is an ecstasy of blossoming. In itself, it is no fairer than the redbud in Virginia, or the dogwood, but part of the glory is that it comes after a New England winter has chilled the bones.

The land has been bare in March, delicate green in April, and suddenly everywhere you turn, the dazzling sweetness of apple blossoms fills the air. Every old gray-stone wall bears a leaning branch of pink and white. And the old orchard is carpeted with violets and roofed with rosy color.

Now and then we find morels there, in violet time. These spongy conelike mushrooms are all too rare, and oh, how delicious dipped in butter and broiled! It is a mistake to hunt them accompanied by cockers. Morels won't stand a pounce; they are too delicate.

It is possible to go outside the gate and leave the cockers behind, but an Irish setter is a different affair. The only way to go anywhere without Maeve is to let her get in the car. She will sit half a day in the car. Jill says she pretends she is driving.

It is strange how all the dogs know instantly if we plan to go anywhere, even if it is no more than run to the village for the mail. Half a dozen cockers may be asleep around the house, and suddenly they are all galvanized into action. Little Sister and Linda leap from the sofa. Honey pokes a golden nose around the corner of the bed. Flyer rushes wildly to the wood basket and seizes a prize to bring us. He is one Indian forever bearing gifts. The cockers mill around in the doorways but Maeve will be already lifting the latch on the front one (which is the right one, of course) and whooping out to the road.

When we are going to leave them for a whole day, we take the most elaborate precautions. We secrete purses, gloves, coats, and scarfs in the front room and close the door. We plug in the night light for Honey when nobody is looking, so if it gets dark before we come in, it won't be blank dark. We shut the stairway door casually in passing by so Linda won't be able to give in to her baser instincts and chase Esmé up the stairs. Eventually we do get away, leaving a mort of absolutely broken hearts behind us. And loud in our ears echoes the banshee wail of an abandoned Irisher.

But oh, when we return, the scurryings and swishings and skidding of rugs! The bounds and leaps and the plump loping about of Honey! Wonderful welcome, and what better place to come to than a house of cockers and cats and setter? It is such a pleasant thing to be well loved!

This summer Linda and Little Sister and Hildegarde and Melody, if there is time for her brushing up, are due to go to the dog shows and try for their CDX degrees. Life being the way it is, the triumphs of last summer when they won their CD's are far behind and forgotten. Maeve is still occupied with her CD, being younger and only starting her career.

Anyone who doubts that dogs love obedience work and shows ought to see the real huggermugger that goes on on show days. We can hardly eat our breakfast, for the small fry are hurrying us off, and woe to us when we have to leave Melody or Hildegarde at home. They all want to go to every show. The car windows are smudged all summer from eager noses as they travel back and forth. Sister's little dumbbell and Maeve's large training collar and the vacuum kit and the feeding pans all rattle around on the floor. Hildegarde sits up front because she gets nervous in traffic. Linda rides on the shelf in back where she can see better. Maeve sits with her arms elegantly crossed and as much of her nose as possible out the window. Somehow she gets the air of a Gibson girl, feminine but healthy, vigorous in a ladylike way.

There is enough to do in May, its own kinds of jobs. The barbecue to open, the summerhouses to clean and polish, the studio haymow to reconvert from winter dog-jumping center to writers' and sketchers' and readers' retreat. And the lawn furniture, which is especially shabby this year, to be repaired, painted or burned up as the case may be.

The garden seems to burgeon with weeds as soon as it is planted. The fresh earth smells good as the weeds come out. The rosy rhubarb and lucent green asparagus are ready to gather. Asparagus on toast with plain melted sweet butter, and rhubarb sauce for dessert, is a spring supper.

Also, we can begin to load the freezer. The youngest tips of asparagus and the first shoots of rhubarb make the best frozen products.

The evenings are longer now, just right for pottering around the yard, although not yet warm enough to sit under the trees. Sometimes we drive through the valley past the little white villages. Men and women and children are out, the older folk raking or weeding, the children playing jack-stones on the steps or jumping up and down in that purposeful aimlessness of children.

All over America, families are doing just the same, supper being finished. And at such an hour, I feel one can hold the whole of America in the curved fingers of a lifted hand. Surely this is our land, families at home in the spring of the year, and bountiful summer ahead. This is the meaning of our democracy, and let it never again be threatened.

How silvery the moon hangs in the night sky above the stilled fountains of the apple blossoms!

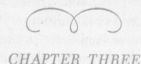

## CHAPTER THREE

J une is a romantic month. It is a time of the year the poets loved especially, and goes well in sweet songs too. It suits Shakespeare with his "but thy eternal summer shall not fade."

In June, in the little town that belongs with my youth, boys and girls walked hand in hand along the river paths, and the sweet white clover foamed shoulder-high, and the gulls swung over in a cloudless sky. We had picnics in the purple twilight, with smoky, sandy frankfurters dropping from the green sticks, and muddy coffee in tin cups. Somebody usually forgot the rolls and had to go back for them.

We had never heard of dashing around the country in cars and dancing at roadside places, or going to anything like a night club. If we borrowed, with great machinations, one family car, we all piled in and drove to the lake or up-river, and had a picnic. We sat around the fire at the dark edge of the water and sang what I thought were the most beautiful songs in the world: "My little Per—sian Ro—ose, nobody knows—how I love you"; and "I'm the sheik of

Araby, your heart belongs to me!" and "Always, always; I'll be loving you—always"; and "There's a long, long trail awinding, into the land of my dreams—" We thought we would be young forever. And being in love meant a good-night kiss in the romantic manner, and sleeping with notes under one's pillow saying, "I love you. You'll always be my girl."

Now when I read all the articles by high-school groups, or about high-school groups, arguing the pros and cons of chastity before marriage, I feel sad.

We must then have been full of complexes and frustrations and inhibitions, but we didn't know it. We felt perfectly adjusted except for not quite passing geometry or staying home with grippe the night of the football rally. We fell in love much the way we dived off the edge of the old pier, just holding our noses and plopping in and fishing ourselves out wet as oysters. And love was a miracle and a mystery and we had no idea we were seeking father images or compensating for something. We just knew the one-and-only was the most perfect human being that ever walked the mundane earth. Simple.

I know now there must have been many a sad heart beating under starched shirt-waists among the adult women, but I didn't know it then. And many a man, nipping the end off his good cigar, must have wondered why in time he picked the woman in the world least likely to be a good wife, but he never mentioned it to us.

Well, times change, and in our lifetime change piles on change. So it is a comfortable thing to have the same kind of June that we had when I was sixteen. Nature can still be lyric and romantic and the moon still the stuff of poetry.

Raising a puppy is a fascinating, if arduous, job. Jeremy, Melody's son, has been the liveliest puppy we ever tried to cope with. He is never still a moment unless he is dead asleep, getting a brief rest before tearing up something else. He whirls through the house like a merry-go-round on the loose, ears flying, tail twiddling, and mouth full of tissue or my best slippers or the bath brush or a pair of good socks. His own toys he piles up in the corner, just checking them over once in a while. But we determined to train him in some ways, since we planned to have him go with us whenever we go. We have learned a lot about training.

A puppy should be shut away by himself in a quiet room every little while. Then when he is older, he will not raise the roof every time mamma goes to the grocery store on an errand. Jeremy can be popped in any room and he will settle down because he is not frightened by being alone. Also, we put a little red collar on him very young, when he thought it was a kind of game, not an assault on his personality. Playing games with the leash worked out well too.

When riding in the car, most of our older dogs spend their time leaping from back seat to front with a hey-nonny-nonny air. So we began with Jeremy by carrying him in his own carrying case for short drives. Perfectly easy, and he will never be a bad passenger in an automobile.

Housebreaking is not quite so easy as the rest. It takes

patience to follow a whirligig and guess fast enough just the time to pop him on the newspapers. The best way is to shut him in a small room, such as a bathroom, with newspapers on the floor, and then take him out after he has used them. And put him back before he needs them again.

Melody has been interesting to watch. Having only one puppy to raise, she has spent more time on him herself. She has played with him until she herself began to return to her childhood. She jumps around like a puppy, plays with toys, throws balls around, skips over rugs, chews stockings. She has taken to bounding up on the wide window sill and sleeping there, and people are always surprised to walk in and see a dog on a window sill, especially a nice grown black cocker.

After this, nobody will have to persuade me that mothers stay young; and women without children should at least try to spend as much time with children as possible, just to keep a young attitude!

Jeremy is as fat as a pigeon, for growing puppies should be kept plump. Too many grown dogs show lack of bone and narrowness of chest from a skimpy diet while they were growing. He is afraid of nothing. He leaps for the cleaner, rushes the radio, advances with courage to attack the washing machine. Anything new makes him decide to see what makes it tick.

Sister Jill is busy in the garden. We are specializing this year in vegetables recommended for freezing. And she is trying tree tomatoes for the first time. The first edible podded peas are served in soup bowls for supper, dashed with salt, pepper, and butter. Tender and sweet and innocent is the first edible podded pea. And how good are the first leaves of the oak-leaf lettuce, mixed with baby spinach leaves and chopped scallions and dressed with garlic dressing!

Jill has been making rye bread, which, cut warm and spread nicely with butter, is supper enough for me with vegetable chowder or lobster bisque. Our friend Mrs. Gee gave us a new way to get bread to rise perfectly. She lights her oven for just a moment, feels the oven with her hand to be sure it is not too warm, puts in the bread and turns off the heat. No draft gets in and the temperature is just right. If it needs to be a little warmer for the second rising, she lights the oven again for a moment, but often it does not need it.

Supper in the barbecue on a warm June evening is something close to heaven. The brook makes a soft murmur, and so do the late birds, and the air is very sweet. The smoke from the fire rises like a gray feather in the violet light. If there are a number of friends, the grill is full of broilers and the sauce basting them gives forth a good scent of garlic and olive oil and red wine.

To have those we love sitting in the barbecue in the June dusk and to serve supper sauced with good conversation—this is a most pleasant thing. And though some I love are not with us any more, their presence is there.

I always wish we were more of a singing nation. My daughter Cicely's Latin American friends can sing at any moment, and sing well, and our Russian neighbors in the village can sing beautiful songs by the hour. But middle-aged New Englanders never burst into song and spend an evening playing some instrument and harmonizing. However, I sing a good deal myself, when nobody can hear how far off the key I am. I like something brisk for the dishes like "Why, oh why did I ever leave Wyoming?" I never have been to Wyoming, but it is a nice tune. Later on I carol over the dusting, "Open the door, Richard." And brushing Esmé, I find myself chanting, "You—you were temptation—you came, I was alone—I should have known—"

Oh, but a June morning is magic! I cut the roses early, before the sun is pouring too much gold down from the sapphire sky. We plan to have lunch under the old apple tree, on trays, and every cocker fares forth to help move the table in the shade. Jill picks a basket of fresh vegetables, the last spears of asparagus, the salad greens, mint from the brook, stalks of rosy rhubarb. There may be radishes and scallions. Also, there are strawberries.

By afternoon everyone has worked enough to feel stiff, and my neck aches like a no-good tooth. But the house is clean, the chores are done, the garden partly weeded, and the lawn mowed evenly. All those unbudgeted things are coped with, too, like the screen door coming off the hinges, the sink starting to do a Niagara on us, the slats falling out of the antique four-poster. Where do people put such things when they live by *Plan?* Our entire plan is simply *Miscellaneous.*

Even if we ever get menus organized ahead, the children will drop in unexpectedly and eat up the whole week's supply before going to bed. Or company will come and stay over. We just don't worry about it; we sort of cook along.

By night, the cool wind comes down from the woods, smelling of damp mosses and flowing springs and wild honeysuckle. And the world is suddenly so beautiful that my throat aches with it. And I think, on a June night, that faith and hope and love will never forsake us.

I suppose maturity might be defined as a willingness to shell peas. When I was growing up, I would do almost anything to avoid sitting down with a mess of peas to shell. No matter how fast and hard you work, you get a bushel basket of pods on one side and a scattering of small peas just covering the bottom of a small pan on the other. I found it absolutely maddening.

But now I don't mind. I like the smoothness of the pods and the clear green color. And I appreciate the delicate savor of new peas enough to feel rewarded for the effort.

Besides, I have learned that the mind can wander at will while one does the routine tasks, which is one reason housework never has to be dull. Sometimes when the peas plop softly in the pan, I remember places I have been. Like Williamsburg when the redbud is a singing color against the Virginia blue sky. Or crossing the James River at Jamestown about sunset with the sun going down in a deep sky and the lonely stone church tower of the old settlement slowly sinking into the first dark. Or walking on the beach at Ephraim, in Wisconsin, with the lake water rolling in pure and cold over polished white stones, and the sky there is a darker, cooler blue than the Southern sky.

I never dream of a place without seeing the sky there, for no sky looks the same as any other sky; the quality of the color is different, and I wish there were words to describe the variations, but there are none.

The sky over New York City is farther away, the color usually not so intense. I think this may be because the eye is carried to the tops of the skyscrapers and they seem like the top of the world, so that any farther distance is unbelievable.

Here in Connecticut, I often feel I could pick a bouquet of stars on a June night, but I never have that feeling in New York, for the stars are remote there, and impersonal, and diminished by the glare of the lights on Broadway and Times Square.

But in the country, the earth grows dark at night, dark is the meadow, and dark are the hills. So the glory of the sky is fully visible and country folk look up a good deal.

Up along the white beaches on Cape Cod—down on Cape Cod, I must say—the sky has an infinite arc, the stars burn with immortal fire. Nothing can make one feel of less consequence than to sit on the beach at Nauset and watch the surf come in under a starry sky. It is obvious that man is small and should be humble. It is good to be humble. To know briefly that the small concerns we have are not all-important.

*On the Way to Cape Cod*

Thinking of the places I have been, I can find the peas are all shelled and I have not been bored at all. And there is a nice panful to cook with a mint leaf for lunch.

Star used to love to eat pods and peas as I shelled, but most of the dogs do not care for them. Flyer, however, will eat anything held in front of his nose. He even eats sulfa pills when Maeve spits them out. She was taking some for a cough and did not want them. So Flyer just nipped them up and ate them, feeling they were a new and different candy.

Maeve has doubled in size, and she can clear any fence on the place with one long leap. She climbs the highest one like a cat and she also opens all doors at will. Moreover, she can stand outside the house and look in the windows, being so tall. When she is ready to come in, she goes to the window nearest us and looks in, tapping on the pane with one paw. She gets quick service too; the old bubbly glass panes might fall right in any minute, we feel, if she applied much weight.

The worst problem with her has been her willingness to open the gate for Linda and then lead her out on an expedition into the great wide world. They were gone two hours one day while we beat about the country hunting frantically. Linda is the blackest and smallest cocker we have and Maeve is the reddest and largest setter I could imagine. After two hours they turned up at a neighbor's, Linda still toiling along right with Maeve. Poor little thing; Maeve had leaped over all hummocks and thickets, but Linda had gone doggedly through. She was wet and full of briers, but she had certainly proved that a cocker in the field can hold her own even with the long legs in competition.

Maeve goes over to help George with the milking in the morning. She then plays with Shep, his shepherd dog, for a while and hangs around to see if she can go help George and Shep cut wood. Shep is very fond of her, as all the world seems to be, but she makes life hard for him. He may have a nice pile of fresh bones from the butchering and George may be starting the truck to go up in the meadow. In the old days, Shep could leave his bones, take the ride, and come back without worry. Now he looks at the bones, looks at Maeve's open mouth, looks at the truck, worries, hesitates, runs back and forth, has to decide between safety for the bones and a ride with his master.

We tell him beautiful females always do complicate life for a man.

Now that the days are warm, we can eat out most of the time. And hamburgers are my first choice, provided they are done just right and neither dried to a frazzle nor running with rawness. There are so many variations a book could be written about them.

When Louella Shouer and I get together conversation usually turns to food. Louella grew up in a small Illinois town where I used to visit a lot, and her cooking heritage is much the same as my Wisconsin one. We can always talk about those hot August nights when everyone picnicked at Krape Park. Which is the worst name a park could have, but is really a nice place. Woods, and rolling hills, and barbecue fireplaces and tables and lots of room for everyone.

Louella likes hamburgers with a Roquefort-cheese spread. We like ours sprinkled with garlic vinegar before broiling—steak likes that treatment too.

Herb mustard is good, spread on steak or hamburgers before broiling. We keep four kinds of mustard on the shelf always, and they all have their place. The Bahamian mustard is my choice for cold bland meat; it is hot enough to burn and so delicious. The herb mustard is good with ham, cold cuts, in salad dressing, as a spread with Swiss cheese on rye. The other two kinds are just enough different

—one is sharper, one smooth and mild. The sharper goes in mayonnaise and French dressing, the milder in club sandwiches and sour-cream dressings.

Desserts are no longer a problem with us. We make up a batch of assorted pies and freeze them, thaw them in time for dinner baking and have no fuss or bother. We like them frozen just ready to bake, then they are hot. A friend of mine likes them best baked and then frozen; she says the crust does not soak at all. But I stoutly maintain that freezing the raw dough tenderizes it extra.

About the only thing all freezer-mad people will agree on is that you must freeze fresh, not-too-ripe fruits and vegetables. Old tough beans will come out old tough beans and overripe peaches come out just ready for the garbage can. We pick when tender and just beginning to mature nicely.

There are a lot of new freezing aids on the market and they are all good. But the best help of all is to keep everything on one shelf ready to use: the wrappers, containers, seals, string, labels. It is so easy to freeze a couple of boxes of something if you have the supplies handy.

Another thing we have discovered is that keeping a shelf for supplies to be sent abroad helps a great deal. When we shop, we simply buy a few extras each time and put them on this shelf, and then when we get a boxful, it can be packed with a minimum of effort. An extra can or two of this and that can be picked up at every trip to the grocer's.

And it is surprising how much better a bacon-and-noodle

casserole tastes for supper if a can of bacon and a box of noodles are tucked on that shelf at the same time.

We shop, too, for the little foster son we adopted under the War Children plan. This is great fun. Roberto is eight and a half years old and lives somewhere in Italy. It has been so long since Jill's son, Don, was that age we have to learn all over again what eight-year-olds wear and play with. But shopping for a child is such fun that I think everyone would enjoy being a foster parent. I like to think of Roberto bouncing a nice red ball at the edge of the Colosseum or wherever he is. With a pair of good shoes and a clean jersey suit on. And supper at the end of the day.

It is the kind of thing that keeps hope alive for us in this desperate time. I feel more hopeful when I look at Roberto's picture. He is smiling a smile wider than he is, and his eyes are bright and hopeful.

Hopeful is a good word. Better than words like Red Menace, cold war, and a lot of the ones in the papers.

What a fine world it really is when right here in our green summer valley a line of friendship can reach across the world to England, to Europe, to Italy. This is by way of being a modern miracle, I think, a testament to the victory of brotherhood over the forces of hate.

I wish I could elect the next President, personally, all by myself. I would ask a couple of simple questions and know who is the right candidate with no fancy politics at all! I would say, "Will you bend every scrap of energy you have toward a plan for feeding and educating all

the children of all the nations? And will you make your
basic effort toward harmony among the leaders?" Then,
being a Yankee, I would add, "Will you promise not to
spend recklessly money we can't get?"

Any politically wise person could knock my questions
into that everlasting cocked hat. Finance, world relations,
economic progress—there are a million or more complexi-
ties which a countrywoman cannot understand.

But a countrywoman knows you have to get along with
your neighbors. If the barn next door is on fire, it is yours
to help put it out. Your own child needs that school as
much as the children on Poverty Hill. And a countrywoman knows the land gives back according to what you
give to it. It will raise enough, if you till it and feed it
and weed it. And plant healthy seeds. And a countrywoman knows that a farm can bear only so much debt
before bankruptcy sets in. And this countrywoman at Stillmeadow believes the world is only a larger valley and a
higher hill.

The leaders can work it out with their superior brains
and experience. But if they have the basic belief which we
simple country folk have, there will be a good time in
store.

The early morning is cool and sweet these days, and
the air filled with birds singing. The flutter of wings is
everywhere. The roses are pearled with dew before breakfast and the delicate gossamer of silver webs is on the deep,
soft grass. The rabbits have been about, nibbling tender

garden shoots, or so the cockers say as they tear out, nose down.

As we eat breakfast on the terrace in the clear gold sun, the whole day spreads a breathless beauty before us. The cats shake the dew from their velvet-gloved paws. The red and shell-pink ramblers are opening on the white picket-fence, and the Silver Moon is budding in clusters of pearl.

It will be a busy day of ordinary living—peas to pick, border to weed, kennels to scrub, cockers to brush, chicken to fry for supper, laundry to hang out betweentimes, a walk to the mailbox with Honey.

A wonderful day in June!

The strawberry man has his big sweet ruby berries ready. We gave up raising our own, because Jill says she would rather feed the birds something else than berries. Something she doesn't have to hoe and weed and transplant all the time. The strawberry man lives just a piece down the road anyway; and his berries are perfect. He lives alone in a tiny one-room shack, and his whole world is spread around him in a small sloping acre or two. He is thin and dark, with very bright dark eyes, and he never changes. We have known him for sixteen years and he is as he was the first day we stopped for berries.

We freeze as many berries as we can, and have strawberry shortcake every other day. Fresh strawberry jam for tea is a delight, and a nice change from winter's cinnamon toast.

Mamma used to make sun preserves, but I never get

around to it. I can remember running out to look at the trays of big ripe berries that were outside the back door covered with clean muslin.

The smell of the juice was rich and sweet, and almost any little girl would have to eat some around the edges. The plump Wisconsin bees were there, too, making pleasant hums. The sun preserves were dark as old garnets and spicy sweet, but I know they were time-consuming to make. In those days, women made whatever was good and never minded how tedious the process, but now we live in a short-cut age.

But housekeeping is fun, and I think the women who hate it lack imagination. It is one job where you enjoy the results right along as you work. You may work all day washing and ironing, but at night you have the delicious feeling of sunny clean sheets and airy pillows to lie on. If you clean, you sit down at nightfall with the house shining and smelling faintly of wax, all yours to enjoy right then and there.

And if you cook—ah, if you cook—that creation you lift from the oven goes right to the table.

One way to look at it, of course, is that women's work is never ended, and I have heard housekeepers say they hate to make cakes because they get eaten right up anyway. You can make it drudgery if you want to, but it isn't. And it is not monotonous either, for no day is ever really the same. Lucky the woman who has a home and can live in what she is creating!

Thinking about what home means, I really got angry

with a hot and violent anger when I read a newspaper headline some time ago. It read: Development Bans Outdoor Washline! A subdivision in Chicago, planned for ten thousand people, was being built, it said, and new owners must agree to hang their washing in the basement, summer and winter, so the flapping clothes would not spoil the natural beauty of the area. Highvoltage lines, dogs, and cats are also barred.

*The Clean Clothes Blow On the Apple Trees*

Take those flapping clothes. I wonder what could be lovelier than a line of pink and jonquil rompers, gay little socks, pastel baby blankets. And snowy sheets, bright bath towels, flowered luncheon cloths blowing on a line have as much beauty as a modern painting, for the eye that can see beauty. Basement indeed—who wants clothes dried in the basement when the dazzle of sun and the sweet fragrance of fresh air are wasting outside?

[ 71 ]

All the cockers have been digging for moles. Linda is also a bird girl, and she runs around and around under the apple tree, in a frenzy of excitement. Maeve, the setter, feels the same way, and the two of them prance on their hind toes, leaping wildly, high in the air. The birds pay no attention. Little Sister runs closer to the ground in her interest. Rabbits or squirrels are fine, but no birds.

Sometimes Maeve is too bouncy for the little folks, and the other day she was jumping on Linda. I ran to the door and shouted, "No, Maeve, no!" She ran hastily behind the big maple by the kennel and hid. I waited in the doorway and Linda went on about her bird chasing. In a moment Maeve poked her head around the trunk of the tree, peeking. She had thought I would be back at my typewriter and she could pounce freely on Linda again. I would forget her if she were hidden. I looked sternly at her, and her head popped out of sight. In a moment she peeked again, and the look of amazement on her face was wonderful to see. I was still there, still looking! We played hide-and-seek for ten minutes, and then she gave up the idea of teasing Linda and started after birds herself.

June is really the perfect month in New England, for the temperature is most equable. It is the month of flowering, with the white picket fences drifted with rambler roses, the purple and gold and ivory iris following hard on the tall and elegant tulips and the sweet narcissus. The white pansies wintered over this year, and in the garden they make a border of loveliness.

I like all little flowers; in fact, most little things. The miniature viola and the portulaca and sweet alyssum are old favorites of mine because, perhaps, it is a special mystery to see how things so tiny can be so complete and perfectly formed. Lily of the valley is another, with every tiny pearl-colored bell so carefully wrought. I was brought up to believe the faeries rang them at night, and for all I know, they still do.

There is much to do during the days, for all the dogs need grooming and trimming and the garden furniture did *not* all get fixed last autumn when it should have been. The weeds grow with terrible, deadly speed, and the grass needs mowing. It is the time, too, to reorganize and defrost the freezer and tuck in the first of the new crops.

But there is always time to carry trays for lunch to the garden and eat without too much rush. Because in June one feels the security that summer has just begun, there is time enough for dreaming. Over coffee, we watch the melodic flight of the butterflies, brief lyrics of summer. Decide the iris must be separated, but not for a long time. Wonder if the fence needs painting—it can go until fall. Feel the asparagus bed is a dreadful mess, but August is soon enough to worry about that.

Actually, there is nothing of the lotus eater about anyone native to New England. Idleness is as scarce as maple sirup out of season. You will look hard to find a lazy yard around even the poorest little house in our valley. But in mid-June we may just nibble one lotus petal, and spend a few idle hours.

Housework is at a minimum because we are outdoors all the time anyway. Summer country clothes are easy to do up, thanks to the imagination of the manufacturers and designers of today. I can remember the days of endless starching and ironing of lace trimmings, and how we never went out without polishing those white shoes!

Now a handful of nylon makes a complete costume, or a few ounces of silk, or a wisp of cotton. Half the summer clothes don't need ironing at all. And the slacks and play suits iron as easily as a handkerchief.

When plastics really come into their own, the whole house will be furnished with curtains that can be hosed off and hung back. Upholstery will be wiped off once in a while with a careless rag. Wallpaper will all be washable, woodwork stainproof, furniture finished in such stuff as makes pouring boiling water on table tops a good sport for Junior on rainy days. It is all very wonderful and rather appalling.

It sometimes frightens me when I read of some new wonder material; I get the feeling that it is just too much. When we get ourselves mechanized and modernized to the nth degree, will we put our energies to work on world affairs, on great studies, on the arts? Freed from the ordinary restrictions of daily living, shall we be free and happy? Well, I hope so, but I doubt it. The chances are we shall still be just too busy to use all that gift of time properly.

As far as Stillmeadow is concerned, I don't need to worry about its being too modern. There are limits to what a

pre-Revolutionary house will endure from this generation. We shall go on the rest of our days jacking things
up here and there, scrubbing the woodwork, painting old
handmade clapboards. And waxing the antique furniture.

Many of the modern things are exquisitely beautiful—
the glass, the silver, the linens, the plastics—and the colors
are used so expertly. But the heritage of the past is lovely
too. Milk glass and cranberry glass and the old handmade
sea-green goblets from that attic in Maine, and the pair of
old French scent bottles with the delicate blue and pink
flowers and the gold leaves—these are things to cherish.

The old maple four-poster with the holes where the ropes
once tied, the chest with one pull missing, the pine comb-
back chair—these are my friends whether they are in fashion or out.

And I feel the same way about other heritages from
the past. Such as integrity and honor and faith in God
and love. Getting ahead, ambition, intelligence about material gains, these are nice and modern, but the old-
fashioned virtues are good foundations to build the new
world on.

After the day is over, the cockers lie on the warm stones
of the terrace, just enjoying being alive. Even Maeve's
wild Irish spirit is calm as she thoughtfully chews a piece
of kindling picked from the basket. ("No, Maeve, you'll
get splinters.")

The house guests—and in June there are always house
guests—drift out to the garden to talk, or sit inside by the

apple-wood fire and read whatever they want to finish today. It may be anything from Winston Churchill's book to the newest murder mystery. Somebody else is always playing records in the front room.

Later on, everyone will gather around the fire for cucumber sandwiches, just to try the last of the frozen-cucumber mix, or cheese and crackers, but in the twilight hours life at Stillmeadow is various and scattered.

Honey and I always walk around the house, trying to take into ourselves the loveliness of June. Little Sister skips out, too, and heels along like a proper Obedience dog.

The valley is silent, the air is sweet. And I think again of Masefield and his own June twilight:

> "Dusky it grows. The moon!
> The dews descend.
> Love, can this beauty in our hearts end?"

*Deep in the sun-searched growths the dragon-fly*
*Hangs like a blue thread loosened from the sky:—*
*So this winged hour is dropt to us from above . . .*

Dante Gabriel Rossetti

## CHAPTER FOUR

In New England, June ripens into July so easily that it takes a keen eye to notice the change from early summer to full, lavish midseason. The nights are usually still cool enough for a casual fire in the fireplace, but around noon there is a breathless dazzle in the yard and garden, and the afternoon is slow and dreamy.

Around the house is a small terrace, theoretically landscaped with assorted evergreens. Now it is landscaped with cockers; every tree has been excavated until it stands on tiptoe, and the soft earthy-cool hollows are comfortably filled with cockers. Melody and Jeremy have a real cave under the best of the hemlocks, Hildegarde moves from pine to pine digging furiously. The result is that our place does not remotely resemble a picture in a magazine: "Gardening Your Place with Shrubs."

As for Saxon, he remembers his days as a chief petty officer in the Navy (Dogs for Defense) and wishes to be worth while. We ought to hire him out to a bulldozer's crew, for he is so big and energetic that his digging is terrific. Catholic in his tastes, he digs all over. He is a sentimental person, as I am, and forms deep attachments to special bones. These bones he buries on the terrace, and then after thinking it over, he digs them up and inters them under the delphinium. Later I can see him sitting, large and thoughtful, with his head on one side, muddy golden paws at ease. By afternoon he moves the bones to the rose bed, which he has decided is a safer place. His earnest face is fringed with brown earth. When he is reasoned with, he looks up with a puzzled frown. "But you can see I have to take care of my bones," he says plainly.

Esmé thinks all this is very silly, but she and Tigger carry on an imaginary game around dusk, which is intricate and complex, played by rules. It involves whirling and chasing and sudden backlashing and rolling around and pouncing from behind the rose bed, and ends in a fierce battle, after which they lie down and sleep on the sun-warmed terrace stones, hand in hand.

Stillmeadow is always filled to the brim in summer: week-enders, the children, lunch and dinner guests, "spend a week with us" friends, and just stopper-offers en route to North, South, East, and West. Really, the picket gate is always open. And there are two simple ways to make this a pleasure instead of an exhausting struggle. First, we keep everything informal; secondly, we plan ahead for the constant feeding that goes on.

Breakfast is set up on the snack bar and guests have it when they want to, and they get part of it themselves. They may either eat at the bar or carry trays to the terrace and enjoy the soft sweet summer morning. We keep a pitcher of fruit juices, a bowl of eggs ready for scrambling, bread ready for the toaster, coffee ready to heat. Or if we feel vigorous, perhaps there are hot muffins or waffles with our own homemade maple sirup. Or baby sausages. If Jill's daughter, Dorothy, and her husband are in residence, you can find Val at the snack bar happily consuming warmed-up baked beans or a nice bit of steak, left over. Jill's Don and my Cicely go in for fruit and fruit and fruit and toast with wild-grape jelly. Don likes a beaker of milk with his coffee. People who sleep until noon get a breakfast-lunch combined, and Jill and I have a sandwich and a glass of milk. None of this assembling everyone at the table at eight.

Whenever possible, we picnic. Picnic is a magic word to us; it is much more than eating outdoors, it is an experience in serenity. This might sound strange to folks who make harder work of picnics than indoor dining. But for us, it is easier and more fun.

For our picnics at home we often take hot dishes, or we go to our own barbecue and broil chicken over the coals or do steaks. Or have shish-kabob. In fact, there are endless possibilities for picnic eating. By the cool river at Roxbury, you can build a fire in one of the stone grills provided by the state, and do nice smoky chops, or sizzle bacon and eggs. There is nothing much better for a supper picnic than fresh country eggs dropped gently into a pan of bacon fat that has a few charred twigs in it. With this I take wedges of ripe chilled tomatoes, sticks of cucumber, sharp pickles, a loaf of Italian bread, a jar of butter, and brownies or cookies or whatever I can find that hasn't been wolfed upon being removed from the oven.

Sunset is the time for this, with the dark water laced with fire, and the woods shadowy green, and the sky like a burning opal. This meal might not be memorable in the house, at the dining table, but served with sunset—never to be forgotten.

And besides all this, if you have the house full, it is good to rest the house part of the day. I always feel the house gets tired and confused if it is jammed all day long. Also the hostess! Out in the air, voices fall more softly, and thoughts are larger. Small irritations ebb away.

When they are ready, we freeze our herbs according to Ruth Kistner's recipe. We pick them when they are just ready to bloom, dip them quickly in boiling water, then seal them up in cellophane freezer envelopes. Salad herbs may be frozen in bunches in the envelopes. Mint for lamb sauce goes in a separate envelope. At the same time we make the herb vinegars. We put several sprigs of herbs in a bottle full of vinegar just brought to the boiling point, seal tightly and let stand for three weeks. If the vinegar is strong enough, you may pour it off into other containers. We leave the herbs right in, as we love plenty of flavor.

We keep a flask-shaped antique bottle on the shelf in the kitchen filled with French dressing, for we have a green salad once a day and often twice.

I vary this by using pickle juice for part of the vinegar, a spoonful of Worcestershire sauce, steak sauce or tomato catchup. Sometimes I will use sherry, red-wine vinegar, salad oil, chives, sometimes lemon juice, oil, mustard. Salt and pepper and paprika and a pinch of chili powder as well as a clove of garlic are favorite flavor additions. I use a half teaspoon of sugar if I feel in the mood, and grated fresh onion goes in with the dressing for raw-vegetable salads. Someone asked me once how to make a good French dressing.

"I put in some of everything I can find on the shelves," was all I could say.

We keep two bowls, one rubbed with garlic and salad oil, one plain for fruit salads. About the only thing I do not like garlic in is fruit salad. It seems to spoil the garlic taste.

With the lawn growing like mad, the vegetables bounding in the garden, the house full, puppies loping around the roses, July is not exactly an idle summer season. I sometimes wonder where the advertisers get their notion of long, idle summer days anyway. Who has them? Nobody I know.

Annually we plan to do a lot of idling in summer. Stop work of all kinds at four. So at four-fifteen we are picking the beans and freezing them, for tomorrow will be too late. At five I sit down in the lovely lounging chair with a new magazine and suddenly there is a new recipe which is elegant. I can't wait to try it. And I don't.

In the evening, that long idle evening, Jill decides to run off a few pictures just to see how well they turn out. I stretch out with Keat's *Letters,* and then Esmé comes and sits on my neck, explaining in clear Siamese that she wishes to be brushed and fed an extra sardine. And suddenly another summer day is gone, and we haven't idled at all!

Next summer we are going to stop work at four o'clock every afternoon and spend the rest of the day like limpets, just clinging. But this summer we have so many interesting jobs.

Life in the country can never be dull. Every day is new, filled with simple adventures in living. Plenty of hard work, but in the evening, when the old familiar enchantment of the moon begins, there is the satisfaction of a house serene, a garden cared for, the dogs, cats, and humans content and a new summer day tomorrow!

Here in the quiet fold of the green hills, we may not do anything world-shaking. We can only dip in our bucket where we are, as a Virginia friend says.

And yet our country was founded by men and women who did just that. And I am comforted by the remembrance that it was not the kings and captains that laid the foundations for a democracy that still persists, but the man and woman in homespun who conquered the vast wilderness.

I have never had any trouble with the law. Once, when I was sixteen, I was stopped by a policeman for speeding, but I was only spoken to firmly. And once I had a brush with a parking meter in Danbury which I fed fifteen or twenty pennies and which never registered, so a policeman collected a dollar extra from me, but even that was not too serious. But I have always been afraid of policemen, just the same. Bowling along at thirty miles an hour, I tremble when a police car rolls by. Traffic men inspire me with the shakes.

But all that is over now. For last week, Jill and I went with Fay to the Bethany police barracks and had lunch with a tableful of state troopers, and they are lovely men! It came about because Fay was doing a kind of state information thing on the radio and two of them had broadcast.

Now I am wondering how many women know as little as I did about the services of their state police. They are protectors, and not persecutors. And meeting them informally gave me a lesson in the value of democracy I shall never forget, for the police system employed by the state in other countries is a far different organization.

The Bethany barracks is a brace of brick buildings overlooking the gentle hills. The main office building was filled with tall, easy-walking troopers when we went in.

"How do you do?" said the lieutenant pleasantly. "It's nice to see you. We'll show you around, then have lunch. Let me know if there is anything I can do for you."

He was a big man, with bright, twinkling eyes and a smile Hollywood could do a lot with, a soft and easy voice. He stood up when we came in, and when we went out with Officer Foley to do the tour. He did not bark, or scowl, or chew his words off. He did not ask for my license, which I had forgotten, or my car papers—or where I was the night of the twenty-first.

We went to the workshop first. There was the ambulance—the most comfortable and speediest type—just back from taking a farmer to the hospital after he had fallen from a hayload and broken his back. We saw the wrecker, built right there by the civilian workers, which could lift a car right out of a river bed or haul fallen timbers from a house flattened by a hurricane. We saw the shelves of grappling hooks for drowning accidents. We saw a lot of contrivances I couldn't even list, for first aid and fire and traffic accidents.

Then we went back to the kennels and saw the dogs. The bloodhounds greeted us with sad and gentle eyes. And right then and there we revised our ideas of them as Eliza-crossing-the-ice animals. They are used most often to find lost people, strayed little children or mentally ill older folk, and they simply follow a trail and lead the troopers to the lost one. We met the star who had followed a scent after twenty-four hours and saved the life of a woman lost in a swamp and up to her waist in muck and water.

"He went right to her," said Officer Foley. "Picked up that two-day-cold scent as easy as anything."

We met, politely, the Doberman pinschers. Now I do not like the idea of dogs attacking people, and yet I had to admit that an escaped maniacal murderer ought to be captured as fast as possible. The dogs bring the man down, when an officer would have to shoot. We went back and said a special good-by to the dog who saved two lives in one week.

Then we had lunch—and it was very gay and informal at the sunny dining-room table. The dishes were set in a service shelf, and I have seldom felt so proud as when the arm of the law was used to set my lunch in front of me, for the officers did the serving.

We talked about dog training and got some sage advice on how to make Hildegarde heel more closely, and keep Maeve from jumping fences. "Every dog has its own personality," said Officer Foley, "and you have to understand him. You can't get anything from a dog by cruelty, you need patience and a feeling for the dog.

"Of course," he added, "we have a black cocker at home, and he doesn't do anything except run the house. But cockers and setters are fine dogs, we just spoil ours."

"Well," I said, when we left, "the next time anything goes wrong at Stillmeadow, I am just going to call the state police, no matter what it is. They will fix it."

And when a police car passed us, I didn't even shiver as we rolled along at a dazzling speed of thirty-five miles an hour!

Thinking it over, I felt the story of one trooper ought to be broadcast to all countries. He picked up a man late one night plodding along the road, looking like a vagrant.

"When I asked him for identification papers, I thought he'd faint," said the young trooper. "Then I saw he was a Pole or Czech and didn't understand English. It came to me he thought I'd drag him off to a concentration camp maybe—he was so scared he couldn't stand up. So I just

*Maeve Goes Out the Gate Like This*

said I'd take him anyplace he was going. When he understood, he couldn't believe it. Guess the police mean something different over there."

When we got home, Maeve and Linda were gone. "Your wild Irish rose is off again," said Jill, "and I wish she wouldn't lure Linda with her."

Maeve has a wandering foot. Unlike cockers who always sit outside whatever door is nearest us, the setter has lots to do far away.

The hairdresser asked me recently how in the world I got three gray hairs.

"I have an Irish setter," I said.

Maeve opens the gate and goes out. She jumps the fence.

We had a crew of men come and build a fence for the long run six feet high. Before they left, she cleared it like a bird. So we put an overhang above that, and the men all predicted that "would keep him in, all right." We had to go to town overnight and we shut her in. But as we started the car, there was Maeve at the door, with innocent, hopeful gaze and a nice smile. So Jill put her in the old pheasant pen, eight feet high as to fence, and we went on. When we came back, George had put her in the garage after she chewed the fence up enough to climb out.

Everybody in the village is interested in us and our setter. The phone rings. "I have a red setter and a small black dog here," says a woman. Someone drives off and gets them, always plastered with swamp mud and Linda with her tongue out. Her mad passion for Maeve really keeps her busy.

We sent for a tag with the phone number on it, and Maeve carries it on her collar. So the phone rings again. "Are you missing a couple of dogs? They just went over the stone fence toward the highway."

Everyone is helpful, too, about suggesting what to do. One man says you can train a dog not to jump a fence by standing on the other side, hidden, and throwing a pail of cold water over him (they always say "him") as he jumps.

"But I can't lurk behind a tree all day," says Jill, "with a pail of water. Besides, she'd know I was there. It would be another game."

"An electric fence will fix it," says another.

"Maeve is too sensitive," I object. "She'd never get over it."

"Well, we'll just have to make home so attractive that she doesn't want to roam," says Jill.

She doesn't go so far if Linda can't go with her. Linda, of course, wouldn't set paw out of the yard except to follow the beautiful flying feet of her adored Maeve. So we keep them from being in the yard together. George fixed the fence in the long run this week so it seems to keep her in.

And for the benefit of benighted souls who don't believe dogs think, I want to say that the fence is a foot lower in just one spot of the whole two hundred yards, and that Maeve inspected, and found that one spot and went up and over just there.

It can get fearsomely hot in July in Connecticut. Some days the air is like a flannel blanket dipped in steam. Swimming makes life endurable; a cold fresh stream is one of the nicest things God ever made. And the sound of water is such a cool sound. And picnic food eaten after the swimming is the best food there is. Grilled frankfurters are tops, with lots of herb-mustard sauce. The long rolls should be toasted too. Fresh ripe chilled tomatoes to eat in the hand are my choice for vegetables. We have one of those bags which keep food frozen, so we can always have ice cream for dessert—and we carry cones and serve it that way.

Summer is so brief, every day so packed with living, and

I hate to see each day end. The long twilights are like separate amethysts on a silver chain. The scent of the Nicotiana
is a rapture to breathe. I wish I could breathe twice for
every breath. It is almost too tropical and rich for New
England, but the plants grow lavishly. When we sit in the
garden and watch night come and breathe the Nicotiana's
perfume, I know the world is a good place. And I always
humbly wish I might share all the beauty of our forty acres
with everyone who needs summer in his heart!

This is the first summer in fourteen that Windy has not
been with us to share the long gold days and soft blue
nights. It might seem strange, when we have always fourteen or fifteen dogs, to miss one so much. But the life of
a dog like Windy makes a better life for everyone who
knows him. He made us a great gift of courage and cheer-
fulness. He was only a small, compact, shining red cocker,
but his heart was a great one.

Once this past bitter winter he got stuck in a snowdrift,
losing the narrow path around the house. He floundered
one way and then another, his ears flat on the snow, his
muzzle white. But he never uttered a complaint, although
many of our dogs would have screamed for help if they
were in trouble. Jill rushed to rescue him and I could see,
from the window, the way he lifted his blind face and
seemed to grin at her, and the way his tail whipped the
snow.

Many sensible people would have advised us to put him
to sleep, an old blind dog. We didn't feel that way. He was

the happiest dog we ever had; and racing around his favorite bushes, he didn't seem handicapped at all.

Dying is a lonely business; I am glad to think that when he had his heart attack we were at home and he had been out in the yard on a clear spring day, digging around in the young green violets. Jill carried him to the kitchen and called the doctor.

His last conscious act was to wag his tail. He went away so quietly that although I was holding him, I could not tell which was the last breath. We couldn't help feeling that he ended his life giving as little trouble as he could.

He was named Windy Dawn, for the burnished fire of his coat, and perhaps we could write his epitaph simply, "Windy Dawn, Gentleman." And yet he really does not need an epitaph; his spirit is still with us on these lovely summer nights and I feel that now he knows that because of him, we are better folks at Stillmeadow—or at least we try to be!

A good place for the Fourth of July picnic is right in your own back yard. For that week end, if ever, the roads are jammed with cars, the picnic spots are crowded, and I do not like to spread the lunch by a purling stream and then have a bevy of small boys begin to set off firecrackers right under the grill where I am turning the buns.

Even the lonely and lovely secret places are hard to get to without threading the highway traffic. It is strange how Americans have to go somewhere in order to get back. And I remember when I was a little girl it was the same.

Fourth of July always found us with the old car jammed with hampers, people, and the Irish setter, and Father speeded to the farthest possible distance for the Fourth of July picnic. We always had to hurry so we could get back to town in time for the fireworks.

The regulation of fireworks has never been clear to me. They seem to be illegal to sell, yet are sold at every roadside stand. They are highly dangerous, an invitation to disaster, for small boys can never believe the little scarlet cylinders may go off in their faces. Certainly they should be eliminated from the celebration of the Fourth, but it seems to me that substituting plenty of safe gadgets would be a fine thing. We all need color and glamour, the oldest and the youngest, and if every community would provide the rockets and candles and stars and fires, with parents subscribing funds for the purchase, and set them off under controlled (and partylike) conditions, the Fourth would be better. Many communities do this, and it should be universal.

Another thing I feel is that we might give considerable thought to what we are celebrating on the glorious Fourth. Under almost impossible conditions America was born and preserved for freedom—and freedom is a solemn responsibility, though we speak of it too loosely and too much. It's a pretty big concept, but by their deeds ye shall know them. No man is really free who thinks a bathing beach is properly saved for him and his own race or religion. Or that he must sit in one part of a conveyance. We tend to imprison ourselves in prejudices, and the Fourth of July is a fine time to consider what America should mean and burn up a few of our old notions in the ashes of the last pin wheel.

This season I finally went back to Wellesley again. There are many women who must feel the way I have: that the college years were so special, and are so irrevocably gone, that going back would not be bearable.

Once I almost went to a high-school reunion, but thought better of it. Those golden boys and girls should stay where they were in my mind, not change to grownups. Being able to see back with such photographic clarity, I could visualize even the lace on the collars of the girls' graduation dresses, and the way the boys' ears seemed to stick out when their necks got tightened into their collars. Better let it be, I thought.

Now I have changed my mind, for going back isn't all nostalgia by any means. I now think everyone should go back to his school and get a feeling of how wonderful the world can be, for education is growing and enlarging, and the future world is going to be a far better place, for the young of today are being trained to make it so. I spent three days being intellectually excited and spiritually inspired, and in the end I was exhausted from the experience, but much comforted about the world our children will inherit, all the newspapers to the contrary.

We must let our culture increase and develop, we must let nothing interfere with education, and we need better teaching, better equipment everywhere. For, as Doctor

Horton said in his Sunday sermon, "What is the use of preserving our heads if there is nothing in them?"

Some things, I found, had not changed. The elevator in the dormitory still stopped between floors and just stayed there. The mattress I slept on was indubitably the same one I had for four years in college. And I still got boiled the minute I turned on the hot water in the shower, and leaped screaming from the stall. The chapel seats are still designed for undernourished giraffes. But the new buildings have automatic water fountains! And the new dormitories are to have sewing rooms and laundry rooms, for the girls of today want to be practical as well as literary.

When I took botany I spent the whole year trying to draw a pear bud. Now the girls learn how to landscape gardens, all about soil, about regional botanical conditions —I wished I could go right back and begin again. How much I could learn working in that greenhouse which would help a countrywoman on a New England farm!

My classmates were considerably surprised to see me. "What are *you* doing here?" was their instant reaction.

"I don't know," I said. "I was invited."

But in a few hours, I found out nobody had changed, after all. And it was very pleasant to think that people may change a lot in looks, but you find the same courage and good cheer and wit and kindness in a person, no matter what time has passed. A group of middle-aged women sitting on cots in the dormitory and having a bull session certainly does not resemble the group of young and starry-eyed girls superficially, but how like they are still! Only now instead of wondering who is going to marry whom, they talk about who is going to marry their children, or how many teeth the newest grandchild has—a very nice shift in importance.

I found Boston delightfully the same too. But I kept getting stepped on all the time until I realized I was walking like a New Yorker. For a long time, New York has been the only city I ever go to, and the gait in New York is like a streamliner on a clear track. In Boston, people stroll along. Maybe that is why they did not look so tired to me. I saw more well-dressed businessmen sauntering along, and more women with fresh country-colored faces. There wasn't the glitter of Fifth Avenue by any means, but there was a nice sense of comfort. I do love the glamour of Radio City and the swift imperative sweep of the skyscrapers, but I also love the swan boats in the lake on the Common and the old burying ground right off the main shops, where my ancestor sleeps. Wonderful America where you have both!

Coming home is the best sensation of all. Maybe that is what vacations are really for, to make the heart happy at coming back. No matter what elegant food you may have on your vacation trip, how lovely to get out the familiar iron spider and begin breaking your own freshly gathered eggs in the chipped blue bowl.

We made Bar-le-Duc yesterday. The currant bushes are out in the small orchard, and the shiny dark-red currants hang thickly beautiful in the green. The sun is hot on my neck when I pick them and feels fine. The sky dazzles, and the air smells like pure wild honey. Plop, plop, the smooth berries fall. Or are they berries? This is something to wonder about dreamily as I go round and round the currant bush.

Bar-le-Duc made in the French way is frightfully complex. I do not make it the hard way, for it is elegant just composed of nature's ripe fruit—and a few green ones—plus the sugar, boiled together and packed in baby-food jars. With cream cheese and crackers—delicious.

Currant jelly is one of the best of all. It is a lyric of jellies, clear and lucent with color, just tart enough to be right on tiny lacy-edged pancakes. Or popped in fluffy rolls.

Picking is always a little hazardous at Stillmeadow, for any moment you reach out you may find a nose belonging to an Irish setter or a muzzle that means cocker instead of what you expect. Maeve is so intensely curious, she can't bear not to have her red head into everything. If I set my berry pail down she may decide to play ball with it and off she goes. But if she is shut up in the house the most wistful face in Connecticut is pressed against the windowpane. An Irisher in sadness would melt granite.

I have a friend who agrees with me as to the intelligence of setters. She was supposed to give pills in the food to hers and she did. The pills all turned up later, hidden in the woodbox by the stove.

The cockers and Maeve are buying me a French copper chafing dish with their Obedience Show money, but so far

Maeve has contributed only a five-pound bag of dog food to the pool. She gets too gay in the ring and the spectators love the way she gallops around, but the score reflects it too. Sister put in four dollars after the Sawmill show, when she went third in the advanced open work. My old chafing dish from college has now gone into service for Cicely, for curries and scrambled eggs for her young gang. And I have been longing for a new one, for there are so many things you can do with a chafing dish. So presently, when Linda and Little Sister have gone up a few more times, I shall have an Obedience Trophy from our own dogs.

## CHAPTER FIVE

Early morning is like an opal, glowing and soft and cool, with a hint of the day's fire in the depths. It has a breathless perfection, a lucent air laced with silver of bird song. And, oh, the lovely scent—of roses, of musky ripening tomatoes, of cucumbers, of bean vines. George's cows move from the red barn with deliberation, mounting to the upper pasture. Shep follows, his tail a dark flag against the green hill. And a file of small kittens is visible, coming on powder-puff paws after the warm milk.

Honey and Hildegarde are already taking the shade of the well house, but Jeremy skips and bounces in the sun. When you pick him up, his black satin fur is already hot. The black coats soak in the sun like sponges. But Honey's gold coat and Hildegarde's parti-color stay cool.

We eat outdoors, while the new day begins, sitting where we can see the hummingbird when he has his breakfast in the blue delphinium. And the best breakfast is new-picked tomatoes, broiled with bacon on the side, whole-wheat toast, and black coffee. For breakfast we simply cut the tomatoes in half and salt and pepper them lavishly, and lay them gently in sizzling bacon fat, turn once, and so to the toast. When we do them for lunch or supper, I make gravy in the pan, and that is the best gravy in the world, with luscious bits of tomato floating in it and crispy bacon bits and creamy sauce. Sour cream is perfect.

"What's on your mind for today?" asks Jill, feeding Little Sister a bacon curl.

We mull over the possibilities. In August all days bulge at the seams, and yet it is a good kind of bulge, I think.

For the work is fun. Shall we make tomato juice, or can whole tomatoes, or freeze those waxy slim beans? Or do tomato soup after Mrs. Hart's fine recipe? Or mixed vegetables, one of my favorites?

Or must we drop everything else for blueberries and blackberries?

"Then we ought to take a picnic," I say, as if I didn't say that every single day all summer long. "I'll pack something while you pick the beans."

"It's a good day to wash all the dogs," reflects Jill.

"And the kennels."

"And do over the old pine chair from the auction."

"A day ought to have forty-eight hours, especially in August."

Of course we work hard and yet how much we have to work with. Pressure cookers and home freezer units and fancy food mills and choppers and electric ranges. Sometimes we stop to think of the difference in our living since the early days, the luxury that now seems common.

I was reminded of it again when I reread an old love letter written in 1712 which Eleanor Mansfield has:

"Lovely (and oh that I could write loving) Mistress Margaret Clark, I pray you let affection excuse presumption. Having been so happy as to enjoy the sight of your sweet countenance, I am so enamoured with you that I can no more keep close my flaming desire to be your servant.

"And I am the more bold now to write to your sweet self because I am now my own man and may match where I please, for my father is taken away, and now I am come to my living, which is ten yard land and a House, and there is never a yard of land in our field but is well worth ten pounds a year; and all my brothers and sisters are provided for.

"Besides I have good household stuff, though I say it, both of brass and pewter, linens and woollens; and though my house be thatched, yet if you and I match, it shall go hard but I will have one half of it slated.

"If you think well of this matter I will wait upon you so soon as my new clothes are made and the harvest is in."

How I hope the heart of the sweet mistress was moved by the appeal, and that they were wed and the roof was slated. This was no fly-by-night lover, although one might wish he had been too burning with fire to wait for those new clothes and the harvest. Still, he would be a good provider, a steady fellow, a good farmer.

A hundred pounds a year was a fine living too, ample

to raise the children and keep the brass and pewter in supply.

What would Mistress Margaret Clark have said if she wandered into our kitchen and saw the pressure cooker at work? Witchcraft, no doubt, and the range the invention of the devil. As for the washing machine, it would throw even the steady husband into fits. Then there is the radio, beginning so happily for us in the morning with Bob Smith and going right on through to the Hit Parade.

Well, it is a good thing to take stock of the things we have that seem so routine. They are modern miracles, these things we keep our houses with.

And even our vegetables are improved strains, oversize and seedless and richer in texture and early ripening.

If only we could keep the wonder of our world in our hearts, some of the discouragements would be easier to endure. Discouragements enough there be—we should not shut our eyes to them either—but if we are hopeless we can never make a better world.

This is the first year we have had a real flower garden. We have had flower beds and a rose bed and a border and a violet patch and a spring corner and an iris planting and an annual piece by the vegetables. But immediately we saw the flower show last year with the gardens on display, we knew what was wrong and began what I call my Quiet Garden.

We took a space at the side of the yard, formerly given

over to casual this-and-that shrubs and weeds and crab grass. This was thoroughly spaded up by the Scott service, a group of young veterans who are strong and quick and intelligent about not squashing the climbing rose. Then a square of flagstone terrace was laid, with two by fours sunk at the edges. This terrace measured seventeen by twenty feet.

The flagstones are soft rosy tones and smoky blue. Then a picket fence was put in to enclose the whole and keep the cocker noses from too much digging. Between the fence and the flagging is the garden space itself, which is filled with succession blooming, chiefly in blue and white with some pinks.

The focal point is a rosy flowering pink apple tree with cypress garden bench and chairs under it.

Now we have a compact garden unit, which can be weeded and planted. The flagging makes a good space for outdoor eating or lounging, and we at last have design in our gardening.

Such a garden takes up so little space that almost anyone with a house and lot could have one, and any man spade-minded could do the work. Instead of a fence, dogless folk could have a low hedge to define the plot. And the planting may be as inexpensive as you wish, the chief point being that you get massed effects instead of scattered hunks of bloom here, there and yonder.

The garden border is forty inches all around, which is plenty of space. And for the first season we bought ageratum to edge the plots, pending a time when perennials can be sown and settled.

When we went for the ageratum, we stopped at Fay's and found Fay and Andy building a new terrace. Andy had a cradle of old tire chains around a boulder as big as a freight train, and he was dragging it out behind the car. The age-old resistant rock moved slowly, fell back, tore the damp earth in wide furrows.

"What are you doing?" we called.

"For Andy and me when we are alone"—Fay waved at the pile of rubble, rock and turf—"a table and chairs—we can eat there. What are you doing?"

"Making a new garden."

Andy was flushed and dripping as he approached another, even bigger piece of granite.

"My, they are making themselves a lot of work," I said as we drove away.

"Some people would say we are too," commented Jill, "putting in a whole garden. It's just the way people are who live in the country. Always starting something."

Perhaps this is the real distinction of country life, as against city life. With an apartment, you are limited, but with a bit of land, you can go on for as long as you live.

The breathless stillness of an August noon is lovely, in spite of how much exercise the thermometer is having. It seems as if the whole world must be still too and filled with concordance instead of ugly sound. The heat haze shimmers like windless water and the woods are dark and soundless.

At this hour, time stands still. Surely, I think, it will be forever summer at Stillmeadow, changeless, exquisite.

With an Irish setter like Maeve, lightning never strikes twice in the same place. She is so big we forget she is just a puppy still, but we remember it when she lopes by with a piece of slip cover in her smiling mouth. Last week

Summer Shadows

we had guests for dinner and it was one of those lovely, peaceful summer evenings. Ruth and Henry had come up from Long Island on their way to Boston. This explained their very dress-up clothes.

Ruth was doing flower arrangements in the back kitchen and Henry was getting something from the car when Jill came over to me and hissed under her breath, "I must see you a minute." I couldn't understand the look on her face, a cross between grimness and despair. We went out the back door and she whispered loudly, "Do you know whether any of the people here have a Knox hat?"

"Why, I don't know," I said, "unless it is Henry."

"Well," she said, "I don't know what we better do. Maeve has been eating it!"

"She can't. She was only in the house a minute!"

"A minute was long enough. Here it is," said Jill, fishing a gray lump of felt from the grass.

"Well," I said, "you can't conceal that kind of thing."

We went back in. Henry was innocently eating salted nuts.

"Henry," I said, "did you have a felt hat?"

He smiled. "Yes," he said, "I got it last week."

This was a terrible moment. Maeve happy and relaxed, eyes bland, the hat a chewed, sodden morsel, Henry all unknowing.

"Henry, how much was that hat?"

He looked surprised, as well he might. Men aren't used to being quizzed about the price of their outfits. "Ten dollars," he said. "Ruth made me get it."

"It's gone," I said. "Maeve has eaten it. Mostly."

Ruth went into hysterics. It didn't seem funny to me. Henry looked stunned.

"I made him get it," said Ruth finally, wiping her eyes. "I told him I wouldn't go to Boston with him unless he had a new hat!"

"Oh, dear," said Jill, "oh, dear me." She vanished to the kennel with Maeve.

"He loved his old hat," said Ruth, going into another peal of mirth. "It took me months to get him to get that new one! I made him have his initials put in it," she added, "so he wouldn't lose it in the hotel."

Henry had the relic in his hands now, turning it around and around. "The lining could be put back," he said doubtfully, "but I guess with the brim chewed off it couldn't be fixed. Not really."

"No. It couldn't," I said.

So Henry went hatless to Boston. But he said, comfortingly, he hardly ever wore a hat anyway. It was just Ruth getting at him so over it. And she had thrown away the old one.

"Now, Jill," I said, "when Maeve gets up in the morning, she is *not* to have Henry's hat!"

"Discipline," said Jill, "is a wonderful thing."

One thing we do know: with puppies around, there is never a dull moment. It isn't that Maeve is bad; far from it. Her conscience is as clear as a crystal ball. She never does what she has been forbidden to do. It was just our mistake not telling her about Henry's hat.

We have slip covers that are very tough, and will wash, on all the sofas and chairs at Stillmeadow. And then we have a way of laying an extra layer of India print over the seats for muddy paw marks. Then for company we can take them off. We were getting ready for a party one day when Johannes, our Viennese friend, was around to help. I heard him talking to himself. "Why," he said in surprise, "this is a very fine sofa when you get to know it!" He had worked down two layers and was uncovering the French tapestry on the big sofa by the fire.

We did have the house on parade when there was one of those tours of old houses and Stillmeadow was "toured." After we had polished and waxed and washed and cleaned and uncovered, the house looked strange and prim. All the dogs and cats were shut up in the kennels. I walked through, admiring the lovely effect. Not a stray slipper, nor a dumbbell nor a magazine anywhere. Clean ash trays. Flawless flowers. Yes, it looked better than I had ever seen it, I thought. I sat down very gingerly, being very careful not to lean against a plumped pillow.

"Some people," I thought, "keeps things this way all the time."

In a few minutes, I began to feel restless. Depressed. There was a kind of empty feeling. Maybe I had eaten too much creamed chipped beef for lunch. Jill makes our own dried beef, and I love it too well. The only sound was the breathing of the freezer in the cellar, a cold and lonely breathing. I went to the window and parted the crisp, spotless curtains and looked through plainly, for the nose marks were all off the pane.

Then I saw a row of cocker faces and one eager setter nose sticking through the fence of the long run.

"Well," I said, "I'll certainly be glad when this thing is over and the dogs can come back in the house. It's too darned lonesome in here."

And after the last of the tour people drove away it wasn't five minutes before the French tapestry went back into the silence under the slip cover and Little Sister was bouncing up and down on the sofa. Honey was climbing to the love seat, and Maeve was standing on the window sill, pressing a moist nose on the clean glass and looking down the road for George.

This is the heart of vacation time, and last year when we went to the Cape we sorted and packed and unpacked and re-sorted interminably. I always wonder why some firm doesn't put up a vacation special of staple foods for campers, cottagers, or travelers on the road. And a set of cosmetics and medicines. The regular cosmetic kits don't do much good for me, because all that wrinkle cream and conditioner stuff I never use at any time.

One firm, I am glad to say, puts out a Cape Cod broom closet which has all you need for taking care of your summer cottage: brushes, wax, window clean, mops, polish. You get everything in a couple of cartons and you can start for the cottage with a mind at ease.

August is a lovely time of the year in New England. It can be horribly hot and steamy and enervating in the daytime. As a reward for this discomfort comes a night that is pure enchantment, flooded with cool, silver moonlight, sweet with flower scent, quiet as deep-running rivers. In fact, I sometimes think that you never get a perfect summer night without having a hot day first. For the heat mellows the land.

We pack our supper and go to Roxbury just before sunset. The water of the trout stream there is colored with

Here We Swim and Picnic

amber and gold, and the little meadows across are filled with birds. A very cool, special odor comes from the pine woods on the hill.

Bacon and eggs cooked over a low fire of apple-wood sticks are about perfect, with rolls toasting on the hot stones at the side of the fire.

We pack a bowl of fresh garden lettuce and put whole ripe tomatoes, crisp onion slices and carrot slivers in it, and dressing is in a smaller bowl. We call it a finger salad; you dip your tomato in the garlic dressing or just salt it and eat it out of hand.

For dessert we can have ice cream with fresh peaches

carried in the insulated bag, or just a bowl of blueberries and cream. Or a plate of mixed cheese and crisp wafers and early sweet grapes.

Vacuum-bottle coffee is fine when we don't want to cook it over the fire. Mamma used to boil hers in a blue enamel pot over the picnic fire, dropping an eggshell in at the end. That was coffee!

The new plastic cups are good for picnics, and the little plastic bowls are perfectly delightful. They weigh nothing and will practically fold up if you want them to. And they are in such delicate pale blues and pinks and greens that the picnic looks pretty when you use them.

Expensive picnic kits always look fascinating in the magazines, but we just use an old basket and pop everything in; no sticking of each spoon in a slot or arranging plates in compartments. I use a separate basket for pots and pans, with an old newspaper on the bottom.

Fancy food is not necessary at any picnic, because simple dishes taste better anyway in the open air, and if you season your food with sunset you have a meal to dream about anyway.

Coming home, the villages are dreaming under the moon, and the old white houses look as serene as if time never set his mailed boot on the flagstone paths. The maples above Stillmeadow are heavy with summer, the pointed leaves of the lilacs quiver with no wind blowing.

Honey barks absently as she comes across the terrace. Barking is just a habit with her when she has nothing special to do. The youngest puppy in the kennel answers with a soft, excited yip, and every dog on the place lifts a noisy muzzle. When the barking dies away, they all settle down again and the summer night is still.

Honey looks smug with that very special smugness a cocker can have. "Now everything is taken care of for the night," she tells me.

And the sapphire eyes of a Siamese named Esmé are shining, shining blue in the silver night as we go in, with another day folded away into yesterday.

The life of Maeve is complicated by the fact that she is the only Irish setter we have. She tries half the time to be a cocker spaniel, making herself small on window sills and in slipper chairs. She rolls her large self into a ball and bounces on the cockers, hoping they will not notice how big she is and will play games with her. Squeak, says Little Sister, as Maeve lands on her.

Then she goes over to hunt woodchucks with Shep, and I see them going down the road after George's truck, and Maeve is busily being a German shepherd. She holds her tail the way Shep does, in a curve, and she tries to run with that slinking motion correct for shepherds. She makes her legs a little stiff, and leans her head forward.

But when she gets excited, she is suddenly all Irish, graceful as the spring wind, wild as an autumn storm, loving as an old ballad. Watching her behavior, I am minded to think that if we could somehow have play groups for children of all nationalities, say for a month a year, in different countries, and do it with all the energy with which we work on new atom bombs, we might close down the bomb factories for good. The children would imitate one another, yet not lose their individual race characteristics. They would be friends, companions.

The foreign-student programs we do have are the best bid we are currently making for peace, and we make it a little late, when the students have their politics all sewed into the linings of their wallets. We should take the teen-agers.

Now August comes with a dreamy haze of heat. This is the traditional vacation time of Americans. Generally it is the time Mother works hardest. First she packs the suitcases, gets the clothes ready for the family, disposes of the last dab of butter, defrosts the refrigerator, and closes up the house. If the family goes to the cottage, she has the opening up at the other end, and the unpacking. If it is an auto trip, she can always pack and unpack every night.

A good many women complain about this state of things and indulge in a martyr feeling. They shouldn't. For what really is better than being the hub of a wheel? Every little nagging chore that means more fun for the family is worth it. My own mother worked like a stevedore when we took our vacations in the days of flat tires every ten miles. Taking a rest with Father was like idling in a cage of lions.

So when we got home from a jaunt, Mamma would look around her house with a satisfied sigh and remark, "My, it looks nice right at home." And maybe that is the real purpose of a vacation anyway, to make home look even better.

Travel has always appealed to me. I would love to go

to the Virgin Islands, or Tahiti or Hawaii, provided I could get home by night. When I do go away, I have a wonderful time every minute all day long, but around suppertime I am homesick with an awful deadly homesickness. I just get to thinking about the way the light diminishes over the meadow, and the sound of the cows coming down the lane, and the way a spaniel nose feels coming soft to the hand. And where, I ask myself, can I find treasure better than that in my home place?

The thing about country living is that there is always something special going on. In August, the gladioli—we no longer grow our own, for a very nice Englishman down the road raises all the best and most glamorous ones. I love to ride over to Mr. Sears' house and go down into the cool dim cellar, visit with Mrs. Sears, and dazzle my sight with buckets and buckets of frosty white, smoky purple, seashell pink, honey yellow, sunset copper. Mrs. Sears has a table piled with deep purple eggplant, and she gives me a couple. I hesitate with delicious slowness over Duna and Mother Machree and Joan of Arc, and then I go out into the hot white light with my arms filled. When I get home I find I have an extra half dozen that I didn't pay for.

People who don't like glads just don't arrange them properly. Stuck in a tall vase as they are, they do look awkward and rigid. But if you cut the stalks different lengths and mass the blooms toward the base of the container, you have something to dream over. The simple triangle is an easy and satisfying design. You use the longest stalk for the line of height, fix two stalks in at the side, one at about

70 per cent of the height of the main stalk, and one to the left and a third as high; you begin to see the outlines of a nice bouquet, and the glad comes into its own glory. One of my favorites is a bouquet of frosty-white glads with a few dark purple blooms at the base for a center of interest. I use a milk-glass bowl, and I always wonder whether anything else could be lovelier.

When we get up in the morning we can tell just how hot the day will be. The hottest days begin with a peculiarly pure color in the sky and with the air very still and smelling sweetly of the dew on the grass. Because I was raised in the Middle West, my conscience tells me this is the time to rush about and close every window and pull every shade, and open the door to the cellar to let the damp dark air sift up. But this is one way in which I have got the best of my conscience, for I prefer hot fresh air to closed-up, lifeless air. So I take my breakfast out in the garden and leave the house open to every bit of summer that wanders in. I have noticed that these shut-tight houses seem cool when you first step in them, but after a few moments they are hot as fire and breathless too.

The big old hand-hewn stones on the hearth sweat on the hot days, and look dark and cool. The taproom—Alice Blinn calls it our family room, which is really a better word —gathers what air there is with *all* the windows open. Jill painted the wallpaper over last month with some of that wonderful new paint which does everything in one sweep of the brush. She used a delicate green, like a young willow tree in spring. Then we decided on soft blue tissue gingham for the curtains to match the sailor's hat in the Jon Whitcomb painting which I am so fond of. And painted the inside of the pine cupboards with *red*. The milk-glass collection looks lovelier than ever against the dramatic red.

The couch in front of the great fireplace is still covered with pink, for we never do get a whole room fixed at once—the way they do in magazines. But the pink is the same kind of pink that the red is red. Then Oscar Olsen and Willie got interested, and made a pine panel for over the fireplace. "There used to be one da," said Oscar, "she yust got taken avay. I make one like old one."

In August nobody wants to stand over the stove any longer than necessary. But of course it is canning month and time to freeze most of the vegetables. I keep the electric fan turned on in a direction to carry the hot air toward the other side of the room.

Most of the meals are planned so I can do the cooking in the cool of the night before. The small pressure cooker is the greatest help, for potatoes and beets and carrots and beans can all be cooked so fast that the kitchen stays comfortable. It is good for chicken, too, and a bowl of cooked chicken helps with a lot of meals—salads, jellied consommé, creamed with mushrooms, or in sandwiches for a picnic.

I cook a big dish of potatoes at once—potato salad, casserole material; and if it turns cooler, they are ready for frying with fresh onion slices and crisp bacon.

When there is a rainy chilly day, which happens in New England at any season with some frequency, I may spend extra time making date *torte* and cookies and cakes and pies to freeze. Sandwiches freeze beautifully too—I leave out the lettuce and put it in fresh later on.

I like best dishes that can be made of one thing or another—for instance, lacking the lobster, I use chicken with slivered almonds added, or shrimp and oysters from the freezer. Or plain mushrooms, with a spoonful of sherry added to the sauce. Recipes that call for truffles and must have truffles are not much good to country dwellers.

Somehow August is too soon over. The rich fullness of summer is something to cherish, no matter how high the thermometer may sneak. And it takes the stifling days to make the trout stream wonderful to swim in, a hot afternoon to make the glasses of Darjeeling iced tea taste the best.

We seldom have a hot night, but there is something special about a very hot night in the country. Especially in the New England hills. It is rare to be able to sit in the Quiet Garden in the wideness of the moonlight with not a scarf or sweater. The meadows have a silvery veil of mist, rising. The scent of the Nicotiana is passionately sweet in the air. Voices fall softly, guests are not so apt to be arguing over politics on a hot August night. There are comfortable pauses, which are always pleasant to me. When friends can be content just to think together.

I am reading the *Keats Circle*, and I have time to be amazed all over again, as I sit in the garden and watch the moon climb the sky, that Keats was so loved by such diverse people. The main thing most of his friends had in common was that they loved Keats; on everything else they never saw eye to eye! Reading these letters of his friends, one realizes all over again what a triumphant, glowing personality he was.

Thinking of Keats in the August night at Stillmeadow, I feel a quick sense of immortality, for, like Shakespeare, death has nothing to do with him. Truly I believe the beautiful does not die, not the essence of it; though the rose itself withers, the beauty of the rose is still there. At least this is the way I believe on a summer night.

Fortunately, Honey does not ask me to explain it. She is watching a night moth fluttering in the moonlight.

## CHAPTER SIX

The day of the little red schoolhouse is gone. Now in September the school busses move along the country roads gathering the hopeful freight of tomorrow's world. The children who ran around like ponies all summer are standing at the crossroads in their shiny new shoes, their red and blue pencil boxes in their hands. The modern school buildings would have amazed our forefathers with their wide windows and big classrooms and separated grades.

But education is a bitter controversial subject in our valley, for there are far more children than schools. The building of Regional schools has gone on in various parts of the state, and a Regional High School would provide better facilities, more group life, better teachers, wider curriculum. Four of our towns voted to engage in this forward-looking project, the land was purchased, architects engaged, and a school principal began drawing his salary.

Then the argument began, for one town decided the

school should have been in their limits. So this town withdrew, and with characteristic New England independence, they disregarded all contracts and flatly refused to accept any part of the new deal.

For several years the whole valley has been torn apart on this issue, there have been town meetings and town meetings, and the state legislature was invoked. Friends have stopped speaking, families have wrangled, and the opposing sides have issued leaflets! A good many of the old-fashioned folk have joined the dissenters. "What was good enough for me is good enough for the children," they say.

It has been an illuminating study of the process of growth in American civilization. I can well imagine that when Bullet Hill School was built, the earliest schoolhouse in the state in continued use, some of the selectmen shook their heads and said the town didn't need a whole building for teaching the three R's. And I feel sure that when the idea of transporting students to school was advanced, there was more trouble. Why not let them walk as they always had? It cost money for busses.

The hopeful thing is that progress comes, impeded only temporarily in the long march of time. It may be that the present beautiful plan may yellow with age and the school superintendent with no school will hunt for another job, but not all the reactionary forces will stay the advance of education.

And when the cornerstone is laid for the big new communal institution all the controversies will be forgotten, and the children who struggle with their mathematics together will hardly know which town they come from for they will be too much engaged in how the football team will come out on Saturday when they play Danbury!

Some future day will even see adult education in this new school, and the parents will go to school too.

There are so many things adults can enjoy learning— everything from handicrafts to politics is a fair field for new education. And countryfolk learn fast, for they grow up with the habit of thinking and doing. It is possible to live passively in the city, sitting in the theater or looking at pictures or listening to music, but on the farm a man figures things out on his own, creates his own tools, studies the ways of nature, actively experiences every day.

Some of the best philosophy I have learned has come from bits of conversation with a man pausing with the sickle in his hand or stopping to scrape the snow from his boots or resting his ax a moment in the fresh new cut in the great tree trunk. And one of the best naturalists I ever knew is a man who has seldom been away from the valley and who had almost no formal education.

Actually if we did have adult education here, we would not need to hire outside teachers; we could use various members of our own village and learn a mort of things!

One of my friends has planned her own education. She chooses every year one subject and reads all she can get on that subject. Instead of skipping around among the best sellers, she is currently reading on China. She began with the earliest history of China, read as much as she could find of the early literature, went on to books written about China today, nonfiction and fiction. She found books on Chinese art and Chinese music.

When the year is over, she will have a sound and channeled course of her own completed and will really know something about China. I was fascinated by the idea and immediately decided I should do the same thing. But I haven't the tenacity, I fear. I am always skipping lightly from witch hunts in Salem to *Cry, the Beloved Country,* from *Listen for a Lonesome Drum* to the *Collected Poems* of Edna St. Vincent Millay.

So, in the end, I have no body of knowledge about any single thing! And I shall never, never realize my childhood ambition, which was to read every single book in the British Museum. Someone told me they had a copy of every book ever written, and at once I said I was going to London and read them all as soon as I grew up.

Nothing begins the day better in September than taking the breakfast tray to the terrace and propping a book up on the arm of the "quaint old American bench" made in Grand Rapids. Even if there isn't time to read much, just a dipping is wonderful while the bacon is crisp and the coffee hot.

But I did feel depressed when I tried to read Einstein's autobiography with my poached egg the other morning. When I considered that he covered the whole field of mathematics and was ready for advanced science by the time he was sixteen, I felt like a feeble-minded child. And as I went on, I couldn't even understand his words! Anyone who ever feels smug about intellectual attainments should dip into Einstein's modest little story and get a glimpse of the grandeur that the human mind now and then attains!

There have been a mort of articles recently in magazines about emotional cycles. We all have them, they say. You go up and down in a regular pattern. So when you feel simply terrible, it is just because you are at the low swing of your emotional cycle. And if you are smart, you can plot out your own on a chart. This sort of thing does me no good at all. Maybe I should have an all-time low next Tuesday. But if something nice happens that day, I shall be skyrocketing up like a Roman candle. On the other hand, it might rain. The freezer might go off and the radio-combination stop. Immediately I cascade right on down off the chart entirely.

A warm letter from someone I love swoops up the scale for a whole day. And one of those beginning, "We regret to inform you that the merchandise you ordered," and so on, is a dampener for the spirit. There ought, I think, to be some other way to convey bad news than in a letter. Letters should be gay, conversational, intimate. They really should be written with quill pens in eighteenth-century rooms, done in violet and puce. The Art of Letter Writing has fallen into sad disuse in our day.

It should be revived, for in these times most people see little of their friends at best; and often, when they do, good conversation is impossible. Reading the letters of the past gives one such a full, immediate impression of personality that it brings nostalgia for what is gone. Keats' letters, for

Evening is a Pleasant Time to Write

instance, are sufficient, if there were never a sonnet or ode of his left. The letters of Katherine Mansfield have all the delicate translucence, the swift bright quality of her spirit.

Most of my letters, I fear, begin, "We are all busy and well." But letter writing takes time and thought. And we all fill our days too full of many things. Leisure is what we are all going to have tomorrow, or next week, or next year.

It is good to have leisure, to walk in the September sun slowly, humming a small hum and picking a few wild dark-purple grapes. The old forsaken pastureland is a dream of yesterday, for surely it has not changed much since the women in early days came out for the same berries to make candles for the winter nights. Around the gray ledge, I may see the shy face of an Indian child, brown as a hazelnut. Then Indians were friendly here, for these settlers were good folk.

The September moon belongs to lovers even more than the spring moon. Indeed, if we could fill a silver cup with that moonlight, and drink to the last pearly dregs, we should be young forever. For the moon has a pure luminous mystery that makes everything beautiful, everything magic. The massed colors of early autumn glow in its light, all the little streams run silver, and silver rises the smoke from burning leaves.

There is as yet no taint of withering or death in the garden, in the field, in the orchard. The world is perfect, and the heart is happy.

The sky looks like a blue meadow full of gardenias, but the moon herself is a white rose. And down below, the old earth turns in her orbit under all this eternal glory of the heaven.

And the pale gold leaves begin to fall from the sugar maple.

I was reading a book the other day by Arnold Bennett, in which he says, "You have all the time there is." Every single person in the world, says Mr. Bennett, has twenty-four hours a day, no more, no less, but we throw much of it away. He goes on to save fifteen minutes here, an hour there, and in the end saves enough time for a hard-working business-man to learn all about art or philosophy or whatever.

There is no doubt that time is the most precious commodity in the world. And it keeps running along, a river that never pauses. I was fascinated by Mr. Bennett's idea that I could use my own to better advantage. I would like, first of all, to reread *all* of Shakespeare, carefully savoring every word. And to learn Spanish thoroughly, beyond small bits like the General going to the war while the Queen stays home. And lots of other things.

But when I went into a huddle with my days, I just knew Mr. Bennett had never, never been a housewife. He should have had a postscript by Mrs. Bennett on just how she worked out all that timesaving. Those lovely hours left over from not reading the news on the commuting train.

What would Mr. Bennett do if he had saved up two days of time and the relatives from California came just those two days? Or if he sat down to think with Plato for a lovely hour and the washing machine suddenly began to flood the whole kitchen?

At Stillmeadow, no amount of planning can provide for Maeve's jumping the ten-and-a-half-foot fence and going A.W.O.L. Or Flyer and Saxon suddenly getting embroiled and having to be separated. Or the lawn mower dying in her tracks for no reason at all. I ask you, Mr. Bennett, what do you do when the bean beetles come in the night?

I fear we shall muddle along at Stillmeadow, unreconstructed. But when seven are coming for dinner, and the pickles must be made, and the dogs all need brushing, and the phone is ringing, and the ironing lies undone, I shall, from now on, stop and say firmly, "I have all the time there is. Mr. Bennett says so."

This is the month of National Dog Week, and I would like to dash out to Tulsa for the big celebration there. I generally don't care much for all the kinds of weeks for this and weeks for that, but a week for dogs is something different. The organization does a great deal in the interests of dogs, and since Flyer and Buddy are Oklahoma cockers, I feel especially pleased that all the events will be staged right in Tulsa.

Our own private celebration was when Melody won her CD degree last summer at Longshore. Any kind of honor you can win pales into a dim fog compared with the feeling you have when your first little black cocker gets her degree, after qualifying in three shows. That day was a driving-rain-and-cold-bleak-wind kind of day, and we really gave up hope, because Melody hates to get wet and will not sit down on damp grass, and the show was outdoors, of course.

The ring was right by the water, too, and little boys kept throwing pop bottles in to make loud splashes right under the dogs' noses. I love children as much as any mother, but the children who hang around outside the Obedience rings at a dog show and whistle and catcall and turn somersaults ought to be put to bed and the door locked until the show is over.

We sat around in the downpour shivering all day long. The breed judging went on under the nice dry tent, but the Obedience dogs had to hurdle and carry the dumbbells and sit and stay right in the rain while the handlers sopped the water from their necks as best they could.

It is true that a lot of work and thought go into raising a

perfect specimen of the breed, but to my way of thinking they are nothing compared with the work and love and thought that go into your dog and you performing the Obedience tests with success. You are doing it together, for one thing, and it represents a mutual achievement far above a mere conformation of bones.

Melody looked very wet with her black satin coat dripping and her small earnest nose sopping. Jill looked like an advertisement for Maine fishing with a sou'wester blowing. And when the Long Down came, and Melody finally did lie down and stay down, my teeth were knocking about and my heart exploding.

When the judge called the numbers of the dogs who had qualified, and Melody and Jill moved back into the ring, I felt that life had little more to offer. Melody, however, felt it had. It had chicken sandwiches and ham and four cookies to offer her.

September is a lovely month except for one thing. It is time for fall clothes. I wish I were the kind of woman who enjoyed buying clothes. It must make life very pleasant to like shopping and to pick out the right things. I never seem to have a complete costume of any kind. There is always a catch in it somewhere. Then, too, I am never the same size three weeks in succession. Having, at fearful cost, lost almost thirty-odd pounds, I may get a nice suit. Then for a couple of weeks we have guests and I happily begin making meals instead of crisp lettuce salads. So I gain a few pounds. I buy a dress. Spartan again, I drop off some more pounds.

The dress is too long now, but the suit just looks peculiar. Just as I get everything fitted again, a holiday comes up and there I go with glazed ham, candied sweet potatoes and green-apple pie.

Jill has no hat. I at least am docile in shops, but she maintains her independence at any cost. She goes into a hat shop, casts a wild, despairing glance at the clumps of posies and wisps of gauze, claps a concoction on her head, and says furiously, "You see! I look like a perfect fool."

"Here's a dramatic number," says the salesgirl.

Jill screws herself around, peers in the mirror, groans. "Fine for a circus performer," she says. She finally settles for a beret in a different color.

Once she was sold down the river on a white hat with white roses and pale green veiling to wear to Don's graduation. She wore it that one day, looking miserable, and I have worn it since at odd times.

I never wear a hat, either, except for things like church or luncheons, and this year Maeve ate a bunch of violets off my best one. Some of the hats are beautiful to look at, but I never feel at ease in any of them. I feel like a rabbit peering out of a covert somehow. But I know women who find a new hat will make life over for them. The way a new copper kitchen utensil does for me, or a piece of milk glass.

A copper bowl filled with shining green and scarlet peppers is a good decoration for a harvest supper. Purple and green grapes in a milk-glass compote are lovely. I like to do a basket of tawny corn, wine-purple eggplant, smoky squash, and scarlet tomatoes for the pine chest.

This is the time to cut goldenrod for drying, when it is not too far out. The red velvet cockscomb or princess feather can be cut, too, and many autumn grasses. Any material to be dried should be cut before it is too far in bloom, and dried in a cool, dark place. We hang the bunches in the woodshed.

The wild asters are out along in the country fences, and with the goldenrod make a purple-and-gold path for autumn. Except for laurel time, the countryside is more beautiful with wild flowers than at any other season in Connecticut. The asters are two shades, a delicate amethyst and a rich royal purple. Then there are white, smaller varieties.

The swamp begins to flame with red maple and our own overshadowing maples burn into red-gold. Nobody can ever explain to me just why the colors are the way they are, nor why they are never twice the same. Every autumn is a new glory and a different color harmony.

Starting to school is a time that evokes memories in everyone. Exciting, breathless moment of finding your seat in assembly at high school is really next to your best beau! The first day the little children go off with a new red pencil box as a treat. I don't think anything is much more important as a gift than a new pencil box. The slim, elegant pencils, the little gooey rubber eraser, the tiny sharpener, and maybe a small ruler, and all this in a partitioned box with a snap cover!

Jumping rapidly ahead, in the easy way memory can, there is the college campus, the football team loping importantly by, the band practicing, and the dormitory full of squealing girls. I never could squeal, but I could listen to the squealers. Exciting days!

Then there is the other side of the picture. Seeing your own children trudge away, stomachs out the way children walk, pigtails or short curls swaying in the breeze. The empty house, no sound, and a sensation that life is moving along too fast.

Or, if you are lucky enough to be a college teacher, the row of new faces in the seats, the smell of new pieces of chalk, the long sunlight on the campus, the reassuring sense of youth learning still, in this age and any age. It is a lot easier to have faith in tomorrow's world if you look at the students.

The radio is always giving awards to special people. Monthly awards, weekly, even daily. Prizes or a box of coffee or cigarettes. It is a nice idea, and I would like to do an award of the month myself. I would give it to Laurence Olivier for the recording of *Henry V*. We were over at Fay and Andy's for supper the other night, and Fay had an album, and we sat in the kitchen by the old black glowing range while we heard the immortal lines and the superb music which interprets the whole of the play and the whole of England too. The battle music made cold shivers run up my spine, and the poetry was more splendid than the sound of the trumpets.

Sir Laurence Olivier may be a contemporary man, but I am inclined to believe he is really the reincarnation of— well, not Will himself, but maybe Kit Marlowe or Burbage.

We are very fortunate to live in a time when Shakespeare has come again, on the stage and in the movies, with a few great men to give him his due. That's a nice thing to balance against the price of butter. And singing commercials on the radio.

There are still hot days in September, so we have salad platters and cool desserts. As long as the cucumbers and tomatoes hold out, meals are no problem. And when the night is cool, stuffed baked new acorn squash is elegant. I like it stuffed with sausage, but with baby Lima beans, or corn and green pepper, it is equally good.

I converted a fried chicken to a new dish yesterday when it was too warm to enjoy frying anything. I browned a clove of garlic in salad oil, added the chicken, cut in pieces and dusted with seasoned flour (I like the new flavored herb salt). When the chicken began to brown, I dumped in a can of spicy tomato sauce, added some hot water and simmered the whole, covered, about twenty-five minutes. Then I turned in a couple of cups of mixed vegetables (a can of assorted vegetables or frozen mixed would be as good) and simmered ten minutes more over a very low heat. I did the rice in the pressure cooker, and the whole made a good dinner with a green salad, and ice cream for dessert.

Late afternoon is wonderful in September. The slanting sun illumines the flame and gold of the leaves, the lawn is cool with shadows, and the blue air over the hills is faintly smoky.

Honey goes down to the brook with me. Esmé is talking Siamese to a frog in the reeds. There is a pure, clear look over the whole world. The brook water is amber and crystal cold. It flows on and vanishes under the bridge by George's barn. Flows like time passing, but I do not worry about that now. Not with Honey dipping her nose in to drink. Not in September!

*The Kennels and the Barn*

Sometimes I wonder whether any other people are as enthusiastic as dog people. Of course any kind of group activity is fun and makes life richer. The world is jammed with exciting, interesting things to do, from flower arrangements to collecting snuffboxes. So I never have much patience with women who get bored.

[ 133 ]

But dogs—well, there is the real thing! I was thinking of it as we drove to the Northwestern Dog Club's annual picnic. There were two barbecue tables set on the lawn overlooking a beautiful garden still sweet with late roses. The smoky smell of the grills and the sharp niceness of onions sliced thin rose in the air. Everybody was gathering around tables set around the yard, and Irma was passing great bowls of salad, and everybody was talking at once—about dogs.

At my table was the Episcopal rector whose great Dane had just won handsomely at the last show. Then there was the engineer who spends three nights a week training dogs for obedience. And a lawyer and a businessman and the county truant officer and a secretary for a big factory.

This is one of the blessings of dogs that is aside from the dogs themselves: that all types and kinds of people meet and form warm friendships with no regard to race, religion, money, or any other conventional standard. It is a good feeling in a world so torn with prejudices.

After supper we all went across the field to watch the trained golden retrievers bring in floating buoys from the water. It was almost dusk, and the little pond was dark and still and the woods shadowy. Two men went to the opposite shore of the water and tossed the objects in and then the trainer sent each retriever with a wave of the hand. Beautiful to see the golden dog leap to the water, striking it a good car's length from the reedy shore, swim powerfully across the pond, find and bring back the buoy, swimming with his head up and eyes shining.

I could swear he never stopped wagging his tail, even under water, and when he came to his master I was not the only one who felt the prick of tears.

"All right, shake!" said the trainer. And oh, how he did shake! Half the spectators were showered, but nobody minded.

There was work in the field, too, and two golden dogs working through the brown meadow in the dusk were wonderful to see.

When we came home, we told Maeve all about it and explained that an Irish setter ought to do all that too. Maeve will track through the meadow and find a tiny puppy biscuit. Of course she doesn't exactly bring it back—you can see her jaws moving as you come up.

The cockers have good noses too. Linda has five little round black babies, and when she was nursing them she wanted all her meals on a tray—the dish had to go right in the box before she would eat. The first thing we knew, the biggest boy, whose eyes were not yet open, began to swing his little nose around, and crawl shakily across the box, and he got his little head up on the dish and fell over the edge. This, he said, is what cockers are for—good eating. He might be blind, but his nose was awake!

The Quiet Garden is lovely in September, even though the summer flowers are gone. One nice thing about having a special small garden for your flowers is that you can remember it like a picture at all seasons. I remember how sweet it is in spring with the white daffodils and narcissus and white and violet-blue tulips and white pansies. Then the midsummer picture has the blue delphinium with pink hearts, the darker indigo blue, and the white and deep red of snapdragons and the riot of roses climbing the picket fence and tumbling inside. The Nicotiana sends out a heavenly fragrance all summer, and the apple mint and lavender and thyme are sweet.

Now in September a few delphiniums bloom, the herbs are luxurious and the polyanthas blossom and the clematis is budding. The little garden is even quieter as summer ends, and lovely for suppertime use. The air is dreamy and peaceful, and even Little Sister's rabbit hunting is muted to a few desultory sorties.

Sometimes the days are hot, with a particular kind of heat that I associate with churchgoing in summer in my childhood. I always reluctantly got into my starched frilly dress and trotted along beside Father, who loped along at a terrible clip. Church was a long way off, and was always crowded. The pews were upholstered in heavy red stuff that grew hotter as the long prayer went on. The ladies waved their palm-leaf fans languidly, making the air stir sluggishly. The fans made a faint whispering sound. They had one side printed with advertising from the undertaking establishment, which was most appropriate for church as it reminded everyone that the end of life was nearer than they thought. I used to nibble the edges of my fan, tasting the dried palm leaf and sniffing that musty smell, and wondering what palm trees looked like when they were alive.

Modern churchgoing is much more comfortable and

pleasant, and most ministers believe they do not need to preach half a day to be impressive. The music is better too. In that earlier day the choir sang the same songs year in and year out, and although everybody tried to keep up, some of the singers always just caught up as the last chord sounded.

I came on the minister of our village one day sawing a big tree trunk in half at the edge of the town dump. It had been felled and dragged there and left. He was sawing as lustily as any lumberjack and he had a neat pile of trimmed branches beside him. There, I thought, is a man of God, for he is a man! He looked cheerful and relaxed, and he was no doubt meditating on his next sermon as he laid in the fire-wood for the autumn nights.

Around the twenty-second or twenty-third of September we usually get the first black frost. The day before, the air grows cold, and at dusk it is very still. The sunset has a chilly light about it. Suddenly the garden seems full of vegetables and the border full of flowers. George comes over to say, "Better get ready, this is the night."

We rush out with baskets and pick feverishly as the light fades. It is always as if every single cucumber and tomato is outdoing itself. The summer squash is thick as herring in a net. And there is more sweet corn too.

I struggle with buckets of zinnias, with delphinium, roses. By the time the moon is up the back kitchen looks like a market. Jill is still carrying burlap and wrapping paper out and pegging them down on rows of this and that.

When we are all through we sit down and light the fire

and feel a kind of triumph mixed with a deep sadness that another end has come into life. Ends are never pleasant. Suddenly Jill bounds up again and cries despairingly, "The window boxes!"

Out we go again, and now the air bites as we stagger around with all those window boxes filled with white and coral geraniums and soft periwinkle ageratum and polished pink begonias. Why do we have so many window boxes, and what, oh, what shall we do with them now?

The next morning the world is as pure and warm again as if it were forever to be summer. And for two or three weeks we have the most benign weather. If we could only bypass that first frost, our season would be a third longer.

The cool and sparkling days of late September flow like golden wine into the bowl of autumn. I cannot have enough of each day; I try to measure the minutes sparingly, for this is the time of enchantment. The leaves are turning, and I wonder whether I ever saw them before, for the colors are a new miracle of blended tones. Surely this year it is a lovelier autumn; the maples have a clearer fire, the oaks are a richer burgundy. And the goldenrod—was it Thoreau who called it spilled sunshine? The wild asters break their purple waves over the old stone fences. The upland meadows are beautiful, a brown suffused with gold.

If anyone now asked me what happiness is, I should say it is a September day in New England. Plus a red setter the color of the brightest leaves, and a bevy of cocker spaniels in assorted shades. And especially with Honey reflecting all the gold there is in her fur and all the dark in her eyes.

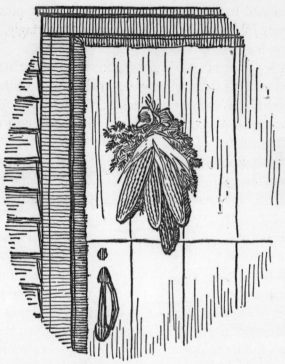

The lights from the parlor and kitchen shone out
Through the blinds and the windows and bars;
And high overhead and all moving about,
There were thousands of millions of stars.

Robert Louis Stevenson

## CHAPTER SEVEN

October in New England is like the sound of trumpets. And I do love trumpets! Even though they make me cry. When I hear them in a band, clear and strong and golden, I immediately reach for my handkerchief. A good band, with a flag or two, reduces me to a sodden state, but a poor, small-town, uncertain little tooting has almost the same effect. Just let that note begin—hurrah for the flag of the free—and there I go, crying like mad.

The colors on the hillside trumpet in the soft cool air, and I feel that same pricking of the eyelids. They are too beautiful to be endured sometimes, or I am too small to contain it all. We need new color names to describe them; all the old names are inadequate. The oaks are not exactly garnet—there is more purple in them—yet they have an opaque look like antique garnet rings. The maple leaves seem transparent, lighter spun, and the gold has the memory of summer's green in it. And they seem to make their own light, instead of absorbing the sun.

For us countryfolk, it is a time of fixing up for winter. The lovely thumping pumpkins and squash, the rosy onions and the reliable potatoes are stored. Apples fill the barrels. Cabbages come in. The freezer is filled to the top with all the summer produce, and the jellies and jams and pickles and relishes are stored in the fruit cellar.

Children are out gathering hazelnuts and butternuts and hickory nuts. The hazel bushes grow all along our own road, and we love to walk out and cut branches for arrangements in the house.

The summer people have drifted back to their other world, and the village store has a more comfortable, relaxed air. No more do slim females in silk slacks or scanty shorts dash in and demand caviar and green-turtle soup. We can stand around in our old jeans and swap fish stories with Mr. St. Pierre, whose beautiful wife caught those fantastic trout this season. Or discuss the health of Joe and Louie's dachshund.

October is a fine month for parties because it is easier to cook when the kitchen is comfortable. Easier for the guests to sit around when they can breathe without gasping for air. And good simple food tastes extra special when the appetite is sharpened by cool days.

We like a buffet supper best of all.

And Claire Moran's clam canapés are the best starter for any meal. Claire served them at a luncheon one day and I ate six. She makes them with minced clams, a can drained, or an equal amount of chopped cooked fresh clams. These are mixed with cream cheese until well blended, spread on crackers, and run under the broiler until toasted. A dash of onion may be added if desired. And freshly ground pepper or paprika on the top. They taste like nothing else, and better than almost anything else. They puff up a little and the consistency is creamy and the flavor is mysterious, so some people think it is crab and some guess lobster and everyone guesses she will have another, please.

For a buffet supper, we plan always on one simple hot casserole dish, and one good salad dish, and dessert according to the season—mixed fresh berries in summer, cake or pastry for winter, light sweet pudding for autumn.

We do not make those fancy elaborate dishes that take hours when we have company. We may try them when we are alone. But my feeling is that unless you have plenty of help, having a big party involves considerable work besides the food. Polishing silver, cleaning up the house, brushing a dog or so, getting the guest towels out, fixing some soul-satisfying flower arrangements—these take time too. So we give up the frills in favor of casseroles that are easy and make cleaning up easy too. When we were making up the collection for the *Stillmeadow Cookbook*, Jill paused to say, "You know, we have millions of casseroles, but what did we ever do with all those recipes for things under glass?"

"Well," I said, "maybe we ought to advise putting a clean lamp chimney over a few of the smaller casseroles."

We have a very dear friend, once from Vienna, who says Stillmeadow is *gemütlich*. And maybe it is the casseroles, for Johannes really dives into them with great pleasure.

Johannes is the kind of guest I wish I could be when I

visit, which is rarer than teeth in a pheasant. I am timid in other people's houses, unless, of course, I can go in the kitchen and make something. Light social badinage is certainly not my forte. I love to listen to it, but I never can think of anything clever to say back. I feel like Esmé, very Siamese and withdrawn. Johannes, on the other hand, accommodates himself to everyone, old or young, sad or gay, and always seems to think of something interesting to talk about. It is a special gift. He would be so completely at home that I can imagine him charming a group of penguins. He would make them feel that to be a penguin was the best life in the world. Maybe it is, at that.

This past summer we have had a mort of guests. Usually we changed the beds as one set said good-by and then dashed to the train to meet the next set. And although there were moments when Jill and I wished to take that canoe to Tahiti that Faith always recommends, still we had fun. It is fun to identify yourself momentarily or by the week with different personalities and think about their lives and feel their feelings.

We had so many guests, in fact, that one morning a strange woman turned up with a large active child and said, "I want to spend a week with you. I gather that you take tourists."

The cockers love October as much as we do. Jerry is so big now, and so swashbuckling. He digs the deepest hole any dog ever did. He lugs the biggest bones the farthest. He gets the muddiest. Exuberant, gay, optimistic, he is the kind of youngster that you laugh at while you fend him away from that pile of fresh laundry on the table. He can jump right up on the typewriter and nip off a piece of manuscript paper. He is so full of spirits that he ought to be used as an ad for vitamins. He loves everything and everybody. He is one long, constant hurrah.

Little Sister and Linda play with him in his roughhouse fashion. These two are adorable, and different as two people can be. Linda is smooth and black and large-eyed and cuddly. Little Sister is so busy all she can stop for is a lick or two as she flies past. She is the first one over the gate, the first one in the hole, the quickest after the food bowl. Of bones, she has the largest; Linda can have what's left. She was the first one up on the cellar door, sliding down and climbing back to slide again.

We often think Big Sister had something to do with sending her to us to comfort us for the never-failing grief at being without one who was so much the heart of the place.

Life renews itself, no matter how much we may suffer. Whatever beautiful and precious we may have is always ours to keep. Losing one we love is possible only if we let it be. Death and disaster, separation and sorrow seem sometimes so much larger than all else, but they are not. Over the deepest scars in the cutover forests grow young, green, ferny thickets. And these do not blot out the memory of the trees once standing there; they are nourished by the roots. But I know people who would say, "Leave the blackened stumps and burn off the new green, it is desecration to do aught else." They are wrong. I know how wrong they are because a black and white dog has taught me. So it should be with people. Death really prevails only when we deliberately walk with him.

One gets to musing like this in that hour after supper which, of all hours in the day, I love best. When the day's work is packed away and the house is tranquil and the evening is young, I always feel a swift enchantment. Maybe it is a return to the days of my youth, a swallow dip into yesterday. I think of what Faith says, "Youth is such a wonderful gift and so often bestowed on the wrong people." Then I think some people keep young in spirit and heart as long as they live. Some people never let the color of life wither away into sterility. The leaves glow in October, they soon fall, and the bare branches lift to a cold sky. But I should like to keep the color in my heart always.

Now the freezer is really full, and the shelves are compact with ranked jars, and the squash and pumpkins and cabbages are stored. Apples send a faint winy odor through the cellar. There are also the baskets of carrots packed in damp sand, and the last cucumbers are down in the dill and brine.

But the garden still feeds us. The sturdy chard and the late beets are fine; Jill brings in a few tomatoes that were protected from the black frost by tangles of vines. Extra dividends in acorn squash make good suppers stuffed with baby sausage. There may be a little broccoli too.

And this is the time to go out to the woods after butternuts and hickory nuts and hazelnuts. The trees spread their flaming glory against a sky like the breast of a bluebird. The upper pastures are gray-green, and the old quiet ledges are warm with golden light. Every year it is as if I had never seen it before and could not see it enough. And yet I have the memory of other years, too; special days when I walked up toward the crest of the hill with special people. The butternuts are dark and sticky, the hickory nuts satiny under

*George Brings the Cows Along this Road*

the green plastic case. The hazelnuts are fringed with cinnamon, and their cases most exquisitely formed.

George's cows stand in pleasant aimlessness on the lower slopes, and Shep and Maeve are after a woodchuck. Maeve flashes around like an excited female at a party, and Shep has the air of a businessman about to sign a contract. Maeve is the color of autumn herself; perhaps setter red was given the first Irisher by the God of Autumn.

I may as well admit that we never, never crack and hull

[ *147* ]

all the nuts we gather. The abundance of Nature's sweet open gift goes to my head and I simply stagger under bags and bags of nuts. But when it comes to getting the meat out of a butternut later on, it takes a special birthday-cake kind of occasion to bring me to the struggle. Hickory nuts are bad, too; the sweet, firm meat is channeled into the shell. I always think of Theseus in the labyrinth when I sit hunched over and chasing the nut in and out, and finally fish it up from the floor.

We crack them with a flatiron on a stone on the hearth, and on cool autumn evenings we bring in a bowl and decide to do a nice lot. I usually finish five or six nuts and measure in a cup to see if they could possibly be called a half cup added to the batter etc., etc. Meanwhile the applewood fire burns brightly and the music is good on the radio and a nice new copy of the latest Joseph Shearing is at hand—and the nuts can wait until another day!

By nature I am not a procrastinator. If there is anything I don't want to do, I usually rush to do it at once. I've found if I don't, I am mentally doing that unpleasant thing over and over and over. But cracking and shelling butternuts is my exception.

Nevertheless, up the hill I go, happy as a squirrel. "It seems a shame to waste them," I say to myself. "And what is better than a nut cake with a Mocha frosting?"

We have some hot clear days in which there is no feeling of urgency about getting ready for blizzard time, and then we have cold whipping-wind days which bring us to the storm-window frame of mind in a hurry.

Actually it is practical for countryfolk to do all the winter preparation before the days grow cold and gray. Painting the screens and putting them away, storing the lawn furniture, cleaning up the garden—there are dozens of things to do. Besides getting the wood stacked and the kindling cut for the long season of the fireplace.

But it's fun to do them, because the air is so brisk and fresh, and it is usually not too cold. It is on a crisp fall day that I plan to do over my desk, clean the attic, polish the silver. Catch up with all my mail. Brush all the dogs and cats. Wash the blankets and spreads. I plan a month's work while I am eating breakfast in the sun on the terrace and watching the light break against the golden fire of the maples.

And then when I go up the road for the mail, I expect something wonderful and exciting to be in the mailbox. I feel gay, in short. Only there is one moment every day when I feel my heart will break.

This moment is one I think all women have, and most men, too, when all the loveliness of life seems caught up at once and you feel you can never bear to leave it. It may be when you turn and look down a country road starred with late wild asters and see your own white house with the yard full of cockers and the red gold of the old maples flaring above. It may be any one of a number of times, according to the life you have and whatever dream is nearest your heart.

But there is the moment, and all the heartaches and sorrow of your life suddenly diminish and the fine, brave things stand out. You breathe the sharp, clean air, your eyes lift to the wideness of the sky.

And for me, instead of being bowed down by the memory of world woe, and various unkindnesses I have experienced, and any evidence of man's pettiness, I remember the sum of goodness. The woman who gave me her only piece of milk glass, the man who carried my groceries to the car, the woman in the store who gave me her sugar ration in wartime because I had a birthday cake to make—there are thousands of little graces I can add up, and all at once I know how splendid life is.

Anybody has a store of great riches to add up, but some people are so busy totaling the times they have been "put upon" that they miss them. Maybe those people never have that deep sadness when they consider that the red leaves fall, the snow comes. But most people experience the same feeling I have, that quick immediate perception that life is a jewel in the hand—and on a brilliant October day I suddenly wish to live forever. These moments are like a coin—with the loveliness on the face and the sadness on the reverse.

I like furniture, that has been worn pleasantly; there are associations one has with certain pieces, the way I have with Honey's armchair. Perhaps that is one definition of home: a place you live *with* as well as *in*.

We used to think it was dreadful the way our predecessors decorated everything with roses and daisies and bunches of ferns. But now in all the shops you find tulips and hearts and birds and ribbons painted all over—and they call it Pennsylvania Dutch or peasant style and everyone gets vastly excited over the new trend. I am sure this has some significance in American life, but I can't figure it out. I am too busy hunting for an old bread trough to use for autumn flower-and-fruit arrangements.

The cockers are getting heavier coats now, deep and glossy. They get a good bath on a sunny day and whirl around in the leaves drying off. Bathing Maeve, though, is an awful problem. For the first few baths, George was able to hoist her into the laundry tub where part of her could be in the water and part just overlap the edge. But now there is so much dog to her that we can't get her up there any more. I am regretting bitterly that I didn't buy that antique tin tub at the Olde Gift and Antique Shoppe. It would just fit her. Jill thinks we might rig up a washtub sequence in the yard with a bucket line, but Maeve is a very bouncy person for that. Pending the solution of her next bath, she gets brushed and her face is washed. Of course nearly every day she wallows in the brook awhile and brings back most of the brook's bottom soil.

Linda has helped her chase swallows all summer, and now they can catch drifting leaves, but it will be dull in winter with nothing up in the air to leap after.

Midmorning is the best time of day in October. White clouds foam in the sky, the washing blows clean and sunny on the line, the smell of harvest is still in the air, the cockers race in the leaves, the cats walk delicately on the fence top. The newest puppies, Hope and Robin, come lolloping up with a pair of good blue socks. Or a wine-colored bath towel they helped off the line. We chose Robin Hood for the boy's name because he ate up everybody's food, a gay black bandit. And Hope—we tell her we hope she will make her Utility Dog degree when she is a lady.

The sun has a bright glitter on the red barn and the white house, and the leaves, the leaves are the best of all the color in the universe. This is a high, proud season, a time to work with contentment and fill the heart with beauty.

This is the time for ambling drives around the countryside, visiting with neighbors. We drop in on Alice and Margaret, who live in the little house built into the hillside not far away. Their road is winding and narrow, and lovely with late asters and flaunting goldenrod. The sumac hangs over it with royal burgundy clusters.

I love their house because it has a special charm. As you go in from the road, there is the kitchen and a family room with a fireplace and a hutch table at the side. Then you go upstairs and the living room and bedrooms are on an upper level. The living-room door opens right out onto the hill, and these days you can step out and sit in the bright sunshine and feel you are in an outdoor room, roofed by blue sky and walled by flaming color of autumn.

From the back, the little house is comfortably shouldered by the hill; there are no windows on that side, only the brave lift of the chimney and the slope of the roof mark that Alice and Margaret live here. Such a house is cool on the hottest days of summer and protected from the wildest storms of winter.

The house had been long neglected but now, restored and loved, it is one of the happiest places I know.

*Alice and Margaret Live Here*

I would be hard put to it to think of anything better on earth or in heaven than October in New England. The world is lit with splendor, there are surely more colors than on any artist's palette, and you can walk down the shining glory of the lanes breathing deep of an air that is cool wine to the lungs.

It is a fine time to be in the country, for the heavy garden work is done. The lawn is green and pleasant and not always and forever ready to mow. A fire in the fireplace gives just the right warmth for the clear deep evenings, and we can still breakfast outdoors on the terrace.

[ 153 ]

I have more energy in October, I think, than in any other month. It is easier to get up in the morning and start one of those jobs I didn't get to in summer or in the lazy September days. I am fired with ambition! Clean the attic? Wash all the cockers? Sun the blankets? Oh, well, I have time enough for everything on such a day!

Jill is working in the garden, trimming and pruning and raking and transplanting. The puppies are helping her, digging and running around with small clumps of this and that in their mouths. They look earnest and important, and every nose is frosted with dust. Bulbs are their delight. Night Flyer Junior comes lolloping around the house with a fancy tulip bulb held nonchalantly, a nice ball. Junior is Linda's plump black child. It was simply awful to part with any of this litter, but five we could not keep. We kept Souvenir too—known as Sue or Susy. The three others went to special people.

At the end of October we may get Indian summer, and these are days to stay out-of-doors all day long, for the whole world is enchanted. There is always a lot of pleasant argument in the village as to whether this is Indian summer or whether it comes later or we have already had it. I am always willing to believe in it any time. And to pack the picnic basket and drive away to that special place by the leaf-strewn stream.

Collecting recipes is always exciting, and browsing through cookbooks is always rewarding. Some of the best recipes I find in those small paper-covered booklets which various groups of women get out. I came on the *Cape*

*Cod Kitchen Secrets* which the hospital-aid association sells, and I found enough wonderful fish recipes for a lifetime. And now that freezing is here to stay, fish is always in season. Who wouldn't like *croustade* of oysters the way these Cape Codders make it at any time?

Most of the Cape recipes reflect the days of the clipper ships or the whalers and are good rib-sticking dishes; they use cream and eggs and butter as country cooks do.

I can remember the days when we ate fish either fried or creamed or in chowder. Mamma made a salmon loaf which was quite an innovation, but usually we creamed the salmon and had it on toast points. I felt very sophisticated when I first made creamed canned shrimp with peas and served it on crackers!

Probably it was the war with its meat shortage which made us so conscious of the lovely dishes you can make out of just plain fish. The mushrooms, the sherry, the chopped eggs—all the things you can do are a revelation. But in my childhood, Father thought anyone who ate a mushroom was asking for the Grim Reaper.

The change in our national cooking is a very good one, and shows American women really do have imagination. Steaks and chops and chicken did a lot for us in their day, but there is a mort of good eating without looking at the meat counter. The Victory gardens did their part too. For we grew to know so many lettuces and squash and types of beans that we enlarged our menus considerably.

We had two kinds of lettuce when I was growing up. Leaf and store. Now in my salad bowl I may toss two kinds of endive, Oak-leaf lettuce, Bibb, bronze beauty, New York 12, and Mayking. And what a salad with a garlic dressing and a little crumbled *bleu* cheese!

We have fresh lettuce, chard, and chickory late in the fall and early in the spring. Jill starts them in the cold frame very early with the radishes.

In a dry season we watch the sky anxiously for smoke. Forest fires are the great enemy. This past summer when we went forty-five days without rain, the sound of the fire bell made us break into the cold sweat of terror. Fires do not start by themselves, and when I think of the devastation a single tossed cigarette can do on a dry roadside, I feel positively murderous.

Last fall we were on Cape Cod driving home when the great smoke pall darkened the whole sky and we drove in a thick gray cloud. The hot ashy smell choked our lungs, our eyes were red and aching. Here and there areas of the road were cut off, and smoky men waved the traffic away.

All modern cars have ash trays, so motorists do not have to fling their glowing stubs to the grassy roadside. Picnic fires can be made in portable grills, not in beds of autumn leaves. If you do cook over a campfire, you should always dig down deeply in the earth and make the fire on dirt and not on dry grass or sod. A bank of fresh earth can be built without too much effort to keep sparks from creeping underneath.

We do not try to cook our picnic meals out-of-doors when we are short of rainfall. We cook at home and wrap the dishes in thick papers and carry them to the picnic spot, and we can watch the splendor of the falling leaves without worrying about setting them afire.

And how beautiful the woods are when the picnic is over and the light is a soft glimmer through the red and gold of the leaves that will not fall until tomorrow. Honey dreams at my feet—her fur is the color of the golden maple leaves; Maeve dashes by, with the light shining on her coppery red coat. A setter belongs to autumn—she is all wind and color and excitement and mystery as she sniffs the hunting air.

And at such a moment, I wish October might last forever, dazzle of blue days, glimmer of white moon, bright leaves falling, falling.

## CHAPTER EIGHT

One thing about November at Stillmeadow. The floors are flat again. All summer, when the dampness comes in the house, the old wide black-oak boards heave up, and by fall they undulate in every room. They were all right for a generation, but when we filled those nice large cracks and made them tight they began to rise. When the furnace goes on, the cellar dries out and so do the boards. Gradually and gracefully they relapse into flatness and we can walk about once more without sliding up and down hill.

We are often advised to rip them all out and lay new level floors, or have them split lengthwise and relaid, but to date I have not been able to give up the handmade nails and the broad, beautiful widths of oak. I like to set my feet on the same floor that the house began with, or a reasonable facsimile thereof. Because I like the kinship with yesterday; to belong, in a sense, to the past. So we move warily until the furnace goes into action again.

I suppose you have to be terribly sentimental to be

*en rapport* with all that an old house involves. For there are also the windows. Those darling little bubbly glass panes look like a dream, but of course the windows have no sash weights or modern fittings. To raise a window you stand by it and heave and then you prop it up with a stick. If a bad storm comes up in the night and the frames once get wet, the windows refuse to come down again. Many a night I wrestle unsuccessfully to close the windows, and then stuff bath towels in the openings until morning.

We have one new window which we put in for an extra, and that window slides like grease. But I am not fond of that window personally. It is just a window. The glass is strong and water-clear and the putty is firm. But the one next to it catches the light in a soft, bubbly translucence. And just has more personality for me.

Modern houses are lovely in the colored illustrations, and I do appreciate the genius of many modern builders and designers. All those wide window spaces and walls that aren't walls but hold books, radios, lamps and archery sets! And the functional furniture is impressive too. But it isn't heart-warming to me the way an old steadfast house is, with its crooked doorsills and hand-hewed beams. Well, one man's meat is another man's poison. A relative from a place that shall be nameless once visited me and said, "I know someone who would simply love this. She *likes* old things."

One thing always fascinates me in the country, and that is the transformation of a confirmed city dweller into a country fanatic. I notice that even most of the authors

*A Vista of Doorways*

who debunk country living have an address somewhere out in the sticks. The first step is the purchase of a place for occasional week ends. "Just a breath of country air when it gets too hot in town," they say. "But we are not going to work our heads off the way the rest of you people do," they say. "Just loaf and relax."

Comes a week end when you drop in on them and they are digging up the yard. Just putting in a few bulbs, they explain. From there on they are lost. In a few weeks or months they come over and ask to borrow our collection of How-to-Do-It books. Their perusal of best sellers gives way to an earnest study of How to Raise Goats and How to Run a Lathe. They go to the city, when they must, in order to earn money to support the home in the country. But give them a half holiday and do they run to an extra matinee? Certainly not, they haven't time. The grapes need mulching.

I believe this return to the country in our time is based on a primary need: to get back to something stable, secure; in short, something to hold on to. For there seems to be no job or position that may not vanish like a soap bubble, and no financial security that may not tomorrow be merely a few figures on fading paper. But the seeds you plant in your own piece of earth bear their fruit and flower and you know they are going to.

There is no feeling comparable to a return from time spent in the city. I love to go, for there are excitement and color and drama and greatness in the city, but when I come back I know how the old sea captains must have felt when they made port after going round the Horn.

Dark days of rain we always have in this month, and New England rains are nothing to toss off lightly. Mamma used to clean the attic at such a time, but attics now have nothing in them except high-school and college diplomas and that book of snapshots from Father's trip to Africa. Yes, even the *National Geographic* left the attic during the war. Gone, gone are the childhood toys, the armless doll, the broken buggy, the school pennants.

We gave away so much in those days. Yesterday a neighbor came to borrow some old newspapers for packing some china. "My," I said, "we haven't had an extra newspaper for years!"

Now it is sad to think of the passing of the third-floor attic, and yet how good to know all those things went out and did some good somewhere, one way or another. A pair of my favorite old woolly slippers went to England during the worst days, and the lady who wore them said they warmed her spirit as well as her toes.

But now, when the rain comes down and I feel depressed anyway, I begin to wonder whether we have all stopped giving what is important since the drums ceased rolling. We send a few packages, we give a little money, but we have certainly begun to be stingy with the gifts of loving kindness and helpfulness. At least, I hear talk around and about that it is all Britain's fault their country is dying by inches, that Russia is a wolfish country, that you can't trust an Italian around the corner, that the French are notably lightminded, that the capitalists are ruining the world or that labor unions ought to be plowed under.

Maybe our attics now are filled with old ideals gathering cobwebs, with old dreams of a brave world nibbled at by mice. Maybe the brotherhood of man is laid away in that old hair-cloth trunk under the eaves. If this is so, we ought to clean out the attic this late autumn weather and send out the treasures to all and sundry. If we do not, God help us all, for our attics and the good houses under them will soon be rubble heaps.

Now that we have our own cookbook, we can really

locate our recipes when we need them. But life being what it is, we already have a mort more that we wish we had in the book.

For instance, *pizza*. In spite of being a Yankee, I now know the secret of *pizza,* and I could eat it for breakfast! It is enough to justify all Italy, I feel, to have invented it.

In town, I used to buy my *pizza* at the Italian restaurant around the corner, and sit and watch the cook slide it in on a big flat shovel. The brick oven glowed and the smell of herbs came out strongly. Somebody was always singing in Italian in the back room, and the whole scene made me feel pleased. Then I would bear my own simmering *pizza* home on a big cardboard. This involved being as fleet of foot as possible, but everyone in the neighborhood could see that a *pizza* was en route and they all stepped aside and uttered cries of encouragement. For a *pizza* has to be eaten at once, and reheating does it no good.

Every warm and dreamy day now is a special treasure, to be savored from early morning to deep dark. The cockers and I run to the door as soon as we get up; they lift their soft noses and sniff, then dash out to see what might have crossed the yard in the night. I breathe to the very bottom of my lungs. Yes, it is one of those days—those last and lovely gifts of New England autumn!

I have the same feeling that comes when I hear a favorite piece of music: I don't want the last note to be played. Or like having the new Joseph Shearing. I always ration myself on Joseph Shearing, which would horrify most readers of mystery novels. But Joseph Shearing does more than write mysteries; each all-too-infrequent volume is a literary bouquet, as rich and beautiful as a November day, and now that I think of it, with the same soft melancholy as a November dusk. I never pay so much attention to the murder or the plot, but I am enchanted by the writing. I just wish Joseph Shearing would write faster.

People are always arguing the pro and con of mystery reading. I myself don't feel escape reading is ever out of place, and mysteries make a fine escape, besides being an exercise in ingenuity.

For my taste, a mechanically perfect tale doesn't mean a thing. I like plausible characters, a real setting, and a sound motive and a quiet murder. Jill, however, will read anything that breathes the air of crime, though she prefers Leslie Ford and Mary Roberts Rinehart. She may be the only living person who reads *The Nine Tailors* over every year, and when the smoke plumes up from what was to be carrots for lunch, she always has a Dorothy Sayers in her hand. But she will read anything at all!

Just around the corner from us murder takes place daily. For Eddie is a mystery writer, and since Ruth and Eddie bought the little white house on Juniper Hill we spend much time over coffee and cake arguing about secret methods of disposing of bodies. And all our friends arrive saying, "I know a fine way to kill a person, Eddie!"

He is polite enough not to say that it takes more than one murder to make a good book; actually, the murder is the simple part of it. I couldn't follow my own clues, I

Jill Reads in
the Living Room

am afraid, because by the second chapter I would wonder
myself what that blue slip of paper meant.

We do get a little more time to read now, for we have
an early supper, and the evening closes down soon. The
fireplace gives a comfortable warmth and we have not
a single vegetable that ought to be frozen "while we are
just resting."

The garden work is far from done, however. The only
thing that quiets a gardener down is having the snow too

deep. Otherwise there is always a little cleaning up or extra mulching or pruning.

Fences can be repaired, new posts set before the ground freezes, the kennels can be cleaned and the runs raked and treated with agricultural lime—and then there is always the lawn furniture for countryfolk. Ours is a great problem because the cockers like it so well. Any canvas-covered chairs are fringed, hammocks grow lacy as the seasons pass. Bits of reed or ends of cypress strew the yard. Only in the Quiet Garden do the ranks stand unthinned, but we sit there only when the cockers are up for the night anyway.

Maeve, the Irish setter, has settled down slightly now she is almost a year old, but nobody could call her sedate. She continues to be emotional, stubborn, utterly charming. The Celtic heritage comes out in her—and I am amazed at how very Irish our Irisher is! When she is gay she acts like a butterfly, and to see her large self vault in the air is really something. Then melancholy overtakes her and she sits with her head up on the back of the sofa, her eyes tragic, her ears limp, and a heavy sigh in her breath. She is sorrowful—in a very intense and dramatic way. But after we sympathize with her enough, her mood brightens, and with one bound she clears the whole sofa and is off again. Maeve never walks around anything, she always leaps over.

The New England countryside is blurred with November and the village streets have a tranquil look. We like to drive to Litchfield or Farmington or Washington, and my favorite time is around dusk when all the supper lights are on. In the stately mansions around the green the dining-room chandeliers are glowing, not so unlike the candled glow of yesteryear. And in the little white houses, the kitchen lamps give a warm family light as the oyster stew is ladled from Grandmother's ironstone tureen.

It all looks so unchanged I could imagine the stage-coach rumbling up to the old inn, the horses stamping softly, the coachman descending with the post from Boston and a package of Paris silks to deliver. The passengers would be tired from jolting in the springless conveyance over the roads we skim on in this later day. The lady traveler with overdress and petticoat in violet and gray and with a bonnet of lilac silk would exhibit the latest style from Paris to her country cousins in Litchfield. The gentle-man, in smallclothes and a fine cloak, would impart the latest news regarding the British over his hot buttered rum. But not in the company of his wife.

I have a small white-and-gilt volume of *Advice to a Married Couple* which flatly says, "It is a serene region in which a woman moves: not so that into which the head of the family is often driven. . . . She is perhaps called upon to allow for the agitations of mind to which *men* are particularly liable, from their having more to do with the world than women have." It continues, "If a woman would preserve the affections of her husband, let her not only be attentive to him in all the engaging actions which her sex, her situation in the family, and her vows give him a right to expect from her, but let her confine herself to these."

Women have come a long way and in a relatively short time. But now and then I think it would be rather nice to leave the agitations of the mind to the men and confine ourselves to the engaging actions of the weaker sex!

Maybe the new styles are a subconscious expression of a desire to be handed gallantly into a carriage and protected from the night air by closed curtains. And I did notice smelling salts being advertised again! What's more, I decided they were a fine thing to have around. My mother had hers in a silver-stoppered bottle, and it was a treat to have a small headache and be able to bury my nose in the cool, quick scent. And when there was a crisis, it was pleasant for a woman to have the delicate attention of the smelling salts waved before her by an anxious male.

In these days, a woman who feels faint is liable to get first aid, which is certainly not romantic. And if she seems hysterical, she is apt to be soundly slapped. Therapeutic measures are all very well, but they lack the charm of the graceful days.

All the thoughts such as these come to my mind when I drive down the serene streets of the villages hereabouts. How many journeys the mind makes—and how wonderful that it may do so!

Indian summer comes gently, folds over the hills and valleys as softly as the fall of a leaf on a windless day. It is always unexpected. After a sharp cold spell, we wake one morning and look out and the very air is golden. The sky has a delicate dreamy color, and the yet-unfallen leaves on the bravest trees have a secure look, as if they would never, never fall.

Always a few late flowers begin to bloom—a single spike of dark delphinium, a small pale rose, and sweet wild asters. It is a time of enchantment; the very name

Just Down the Road

Indian summer has magic in it. Surely the vanished people walk again in our woods, and lost camp fires flicker at twilight by the cool water of the stream.

As long as it lasts, we live in the dream. Almost any chore can be put off to another time; we talk idly of the fact that storm windows ought to be washed, that the freezer really needs defrosting, that there is undoubtedly a leak in that upstairs pipe. But we sit in the garden instead, having afternoon tea with cinnamon toast and watching the puppies play with windfall apples.

At night we take a small drive around some back country road, and everything is beautiful and strange in the evening light. An idle hay wagon by a red barn, an important white hen scuttling across the road, a farm woman calling from the lighted kitchen door of an old white house, a rabbit running to the thicket—they are all endowed with beauty.

Sometimes we see a deer, stepping lightly from the shadows. The shy dark eyes look at us, there is a moment of stillness, the delicate ears twitch, then there is a lovely leap, and the deer is away into the deepening safety of the woods. I say a special prayer for its life as we slowly drive on.

Of course we know this will not last, this summer in autumn. Jill is getting the bird feeders ready, for soon the yard will be full of hungry guests. Our best feeder is one George Bennet, our mailman, made from an old oil can. Two sides of the can make a roof, and the shelf underneath holds a goodly quantity of food. It is easy to move around, and the birds love it. Then we hang suet in a cage on the tree trunk. And finally Jill mixes bird food with melted suet or fat and pours it into small tin cans such as baby-food cans. When it hardens, the end of the can is cut out with the can opener and the can is hung by a string from a branch. There is always a bird having a buffet meal at that counter!

Often at night I hear an owl out in the far meadow. Owls seem to belong to autumn somehow. I always think of what Thoreau said about them, "they represent the stark twilight and unsatisfied thoughts which all have." This may be why the call of a hunting owl sounds so mournful to so many people. I suppose it never occurs to the owl to change his voice!

They remind me of some people who never find things quite right; there is always something lacking in any experience or anything they may have. We all have our stark twilights, but, if we keep our capacity to enjoy life well exercised, the twilights end.

On these benign days, we eat all our meals outside. This past summer the old barbecue fireplace finally fell into a slant worse than the leaning tower, since its feet were bedded in swampy soil. We had to take it down, and with it went many memories of steak and chicken roasts, shishkabobs, lobster broils. I did not look as the great stones went, and it was several days before I ventured to the barbecue itself. By then Willie and Oscar had put screening neatly over the hole and the furniture was back in place, and the whole summer house was trim and pleasant.

Since we could hardly move the building, we had to forego another fireplace, and we finally bought a portable barbecue on wheels. I have to admit, although I am always allergic to change, that the new contraption is a wonder. For we can move our cooking to any warm sunny spot, and we can make a very small charcoal fire for a few hamburgers instead of always having a conflagration the size of an office building. It is a real joy to sit under the maple trees and have dinner merrily cooking right at hand.

Broilers split and grilled are delicious. We baste them with barbecue sauce and eat them as they drip with goodness. Last week we had some particularly delicious ones, and Jill made the sauce. I asked her what she had in it and she said, "I just used the rest of the garlic dressing and threw in the odds and ends of mustard and horseradish and catchup and stuff. Ice box needed cleaning out."

So I decided the very best barbecue sauce is a clean-out sauce.

While we were away two weeks this summer, Jill's son Don and our friend Johannes kept bachelor house.

Johannes is a really inspired cook, and Don felt he could contribute scrambled eggs and bacon and chocolate milkshakes to their menu. They lived marvelously well, but they did have a few minor difficulties. Don experimented with a salad dressing to which he added a few drops of oil of peppermint, and they said it had a rather drugstore taste.

They tried the new monosodium glutamate too and reported it did nothing for coffee! And then there was the broiling day when they were in the mood for Vichyssoise. Johannes filled the sink with potatoes and peeled like mad. Don decided to use the liquidizer to save time, so he threw the potatoes in in hunks, with no liquid, of course, and potatoes began bobbing all over the kitchen while the poor machine smelled and smoked. In the end, they had to use the dishpan for the sort of mash they had evolved, for nothing else was large enough.

They turned the stove on to simmer and kept going to the kitchen and tasting it every little while. It stayed raw, said Johannes, absolutely raw! So they went out to play ping-pong and the game got very exciting, and when they finally came back in their Vichyssoise was cooking and no mistake about it. They scraped off the burned parts and began again.

Eventually they had a gallon of Vichyssoise, so they ate it every day until they got tired of it and then froze the rest.

We told them the dogs could sleep in the kennel. Johannes made one attempt to lead Honey out for the night, but he said he felt too much as if he were leading Marie Antoinette to the guillotine, so that ended that. Then Melody went under my bed around supper time, so they left her in. Then they felt Snow was such a sweet lady she ought to be in too. And then it came to them that they were being unfair to the male sex, so Buddy moved in. And it was a pity to hurt poor Hildegarde's sensitive feelings—anyway, when we got back the house had a dog at every window and a paw on every chair.

Esmé fared well, for she assailed each boy as he rose and claimed she had not had her breakfast. She had two breakfasts every day as a result of her planning.

Linda and the puppies, Night Flyer Junior and Souvenir, went with us, just in case we got homesick. The puppies were then, and are still, at the stage where they riot over everything, and Jill says the only thing they haven't gotten around to yet is marking the walls up with crayon.

[ *173* ]

They all wanted to help me fry chicken the day we got home, but I decided I would do better alone. I really enjoy frying chicken, the way I do it. There are, of course, many ways to fry chicken. I am not a fanatic about batter versus flour, crumbs versus egg and milk.

My recipe calls for a chair beside the stove, one of those high perches, a simmering iron spider, the chicken and whatever, and a copy of the *Saturday Review of Literature*. As the fat gets just hot enough but not too hot, I begin with John Mason Brown and the first chicken.

I turn, and read, and sniff the good browning smell, and savor the good articles. "Wholly imagined experience," says Mr. Hackett, "has a kind of salience."

Now there is a fine new word. Salient I am well used to, but salience is new—I add another wing to the pan, lower the heat, and go back to Mr. Hackett. I agree with him happily that writing based on actual events lacks the greatness of purely created material. *The Red Badge of Courage,* he says, one of the great war books, was written entirely from imagination. But many of the modern war books are rather like fictionalized accounts.

Indeed it is true that the great classics were not reporting, but were a distillation from life. (More salt and pepper on the breast pieces, a nibble of liver, and more of Mr. Hackett.)

While I make the gravy I agree with Mr. Hackett that no book is great for the tragedy of events, but that the people must be important to whom the event happens. In other words, we have to care about the characters. A good many modern-day books fail because the characters are so trivial, so degenerate, or so futile that it just can't matter to us whether they live or die in those slick book jackets.

But we can still be moved by the experiences of Lord Jim or Heathcliff or Kristin Lavransdatter. For we feel them as human beings with whom we have some common traits. They live for us, and we care about the events of their lives.

Mr. Cozzens' *Guard of Honor* gave me that feeling as much as any book I have read this year. There is a compassion, a largeness of understanding with which he views his characters, that lifts the book high in the ranks of the war books.

By the time I finish my reflections the gravy is done, and Maeve is standing by for her portion. She loves chicken gravy poured over kibbles for a snack, and she always gets it too.

The cockers are getting extra suet in their meals, and they are thriving on it. Soon the cod-liver oil season will be on again, and many a slightly fishy muzzle will press against my knee. Little Sister is not very fond of the taste, but Linda loves it. Honey, of course, will eat anything that is in a bowl or in the hand. So will Flyer and Buddy.

But Maeve has always been difficult to feed, and we are forever trying to put weight on her. Jill finds it difficult, too, to get on the bathroom scale with one large setter in her arms and get off and get the weight measured. The thing just shoots up and down, she says.

We were dreadfully shocked to hear from a friend in Canada that she had lost some of her best dogs because an antifreeze preparation had been tipped from the table and they had lapped it up. There was no antidote published on the label, and the company could not be reached before most of the dogs were dead. If they had known the correct antidote, all of the dogs might have been saved, most of them certainly.

I always thought there was a law requiring the labels of poison materials to be supplied with antidotes. Secret ingredients are all very well, but when I think of this tragedy, it seems like murder. True, the antifreeze was not a food nor a medicine and was not meant for consumption; on the other hand it was very sweet and tasted good, and almost any young child would have thought so too.

It would be well for all women to investigate the law in their own states and check on how many death-dealing products are not safeguarded by correct labeling.

I have a friend who works for a company that manufactures many household preparations, and they have all been made nonpoisonous; for, she says, "People seem to eat metal polish and wash their hair with germ killer and brush their teeth with silver cleaner, so our president decided we would make everything safe!"

Thanksgiving is our own American festival, and I dearly love it. I like the traditional food, nothing new or fancy. I like the table decorated with red corn and acorn squash. I like the turkey on a big old-fashioned platter surrounded by glazed onions. And the mashed potatoes fluffy as a young cloud. The dressing must be plentiful and full of good herbs. And our own cranberry sauce, delicate ruby and not stiff at all. The pie should have a flaky crust and be hot as fire.

Thanksgiving is also a family holiday, even more in some ways than Christmas.

*Hay is Stacked for the Winter*

Here in the valley we have a pleasant custom. One neighbor has the big dinner and another has the evening cold-turkey supper. There may be eighteen gathered around at one house and a few more added before the next party.

As the days grow shorter, there is plenty to do to get ready for the long cold. Every warm day, toward the end of the month, is like a gift. Pruning and mulching and cleaning the garden fill the days full, and then there are those inevitable storm windows! We have once more numbered them all. I think this is the sixth time they have been numbered, and I know no good will come of it, but we always try. One trouble is remembering which window we decided to call the No. 1.

On a warm evening, the hills and valleys are quiet now, with all the countless summer voices still. Only a fox barks or a hunting owl cries. Honey likes to amble up the road smelling thoughtfully along the dry grasses, and Linda and Little Sister scurry among the last leaves. The stars are quiet and dreamy, the brook makes no sound.

Autumn is on the land.

## CHAPTER NINE

$B$y December the valley people are really dug in for winter. Wood is piled high in sheds, cabbages and potatoes are binned in the cellars, and squash and apples are stored. Shelves of canned fruits and vegetables load every fruit closet. Evergreen branches banked around the houses give a natural and beautiful insulation against the cold.

The breath of the cows smokes in the morning air. When George comes to feed the dogs, he stamps his boots on the floor and snow crystals fall. The kennel heater is turned up, but the cockers seldom stay inside; they dash around in the new clean snow, barking with excitement. Linda and Little Sister take little nips of snow as they run. How curious that this stuff melts in their warm little mouths and it is only water!

The cats step lightly along the fence. Tigger seems to like it; his heavy black coat glistens with snow, his face is bland. But Esmé's sapphire eyes are scornful. After a brief scouting expedition she goes back to the edge of the open fire and almost scorches herself. If the fire blazes too high, she retires to the top of a radiator and cooks pleasantly. The amount of heat a Siamese can endure is simply wonderful.

Our own cellar now is filled. The acorn squash ran slightly amuck last summer and we stored 125, besides some butternut variety. Fortunately we like squash, especially stuffed with beef, fish, sausages, or even chili! I always steam them first until they are almost tender when pierced with a fork, then stuff and bake until the stuffing sizzles nicely. It takes about half an hour for most things. It is possible to bake the acorns by splitting them and turning them upside down for the first thirty minutes, then right side up for thirty more, but I think they are tenderer with the preliminary steaming.

We have a shelf of red cabbage canned the sweet-and-sour way, which is an experiment, and a successful one. We followed a regular recipe for the German sweet-and-sour cabbage, then processed the jars in the pressure cooker for thirty minutes at ten pounds. We like it especially with pot roast or pork. And the rich purple-red looks so good in a milk-glass bowl.

The freezer is full too. All those hot days we spent putting down spinach and chard and zucchini and eggplant are worth it now. We froze barbecue sauce, too, and when the freezer was full, we canned some. We did chickens and ducks and fillet of flounder.

And nothing tastes better than a delicate fillet of flounder when it is one you caught yourself, because even in the midst of a blizzard it brings back memories of a blue ocean, sea gulls flying, and the good pull of the line when the fish is on. I like it best rolled in corn meal and fried in half bacon fat and half butter or margarine. Breakfast is the time to eat it, with toast made on a long fork over the open fire.

There is a peculiar satisfaction to country living in winter; that sense of being snugged down against the weather must be an old feeling we inherit from our forefathers. Let the snow fall, let the wind howl—and it does howl—but we are secure. Sometimes we even have a sense of pride when a storm is very bad. "Never knew a worse one," says George happily; and "We are getting some weather now," says Mr. Bennet as the mail car rocks in the drifts.

During the great winter we couldn't make it with anything short of skis or snowshoes. And here is a curious thing about the powers of Nature. All during that terrible winter everyone complained and suffered, but as soon as it was over a faint pride crept into our voices as we mentioned it. By June, the winter had become a wondrous thing, as indeed it was, and by fall everyone said proudly, "That was a winter hard to beat!"

I believe man takes a deep joy in the conflict with Nature's worst hours, probably because we feel the glory of surviving no matter how the winds howl and the snow piles up, or when the long drought sets in and water is as precious as a diamond drop.

There are plenty of places on this old rolling earth where man never has to battle Nature, she is bland and amiable, and one might think all mankind would rush to these places and live there. But they don't. Instead, when the flood waters roll back, the refugees return and begin shoveling the silt and muck away. They plant their next year's tomatoes in the same plot, and they still keep the grand piano or the radio on the lower floor! In the hurricane sections, the families emerge from the storm cellar and go out to the cornfields again.

My friend Ethel, who grew up in a district in the Midwest where tornadoes seem to nest, said once, "I spent half my life in the storm cellar, but we never thought too much about it."

It is good to think about the simple bravery of plain ordinary men and women; there is much good in us, I think, that nobody puts in newspaper headlines.

With regard to newspapers and news hours, there are times in winter when we do not get our paper and the electric current is off. There is, then, a little time in which our world is only the snowy valley and the deep sky and our own concerns with cockers and cats and keeping the pipes thawed. We have a big apple-wood fire in the fireplace and eat hot chowder for supper, and it is wonderfully peaceful.

In the early days, when the only news came by horseback once a week, people were fortunate in a way. The shot heard round the world at Concord took quite a time getting itself heard! Today the echo has not died in an outpost of Arabia before we have it on our radio, sandwiched neatly between an ad for wine and a threat to our falling hair.

There are many delights in winter, and eating in front

of the fire is one of them. I love soup, and soup belongs
to winter primarily, though the cold soup is all very well
in August. We simmer a soup bone and add almost any
vegetables left over, plus rice or noodles, so the soup *du
jour* is never the same. My favorite trick is to turn into
our soup a can of some different kind as an added fillip.

Last summer, for instance, I used up the last tomatoes
in a soup, with celery leaves, onion, green pepper and a
clove of garlic. I simmered this a long time, put it through
a food mill and had a rich condensed tomato stock which
I canned. Now we have this with a can of condensed
chicken soup added and it is a superb winter-night soup.

Winter evenings are fine for women who can sew. I
decided a year ago that I would try to make a luncheon
set. My theory was that when we were sitting and visiting,
I could be accomplishing something at the same time.
Going on the second winter, I am still putting red crabs
and lobsters on yellow mats.

All I know how to do is cross stitch, so it is a cross-stitch
pattern. I think I learned this difficult stitch in eighth
grade.

Last week we were spending the evening with some
friends, one of whom is an accomplished artist at all kinds
of handicrafts, from stenciling to rug hooking. I was bend-
ing happily over a crab when she looked at my rumpled
bunch of material. "It is nice to embroider," she said
thoughtfully. "I used to do a lot of it. Of course it isn't
worth the effort unless you make your own designs, and
use your own color schemes."

My needle paused in mid-air over my crab, and I sighed. I could not design a plain ivy leaf, let alone anything intricate. Well, I thought, whacking my needle through again, it is a perfectly sweet crab anyway. I hope to have the set finished by Christmas. I think a buffet supper with sea food à la king served in the blue Leeds, with my lively red seafolk tastefully lying underneath, will be very satisfying. To me, anyhow.

But oh, how I love to look at the table coverings in the big shops in the city! If I could really sew, I, too, would have those pale cinnamon-brown organdy cloths with the edgings of delicate green, or the faint gold ones with appliquéd leaves and flowers of organdy on them. I would be very careful not to hang them on the line when the puppies were out too!

There is nothing so much fun for a puppy as swinging on the washing. And almost any time in summer, you can look out and see Maeve picking off an unstable sock and whipping away with it. When she has it down she lets two cockers play tug of war with it.

We have a little trouble with the cockers these days, for a whole kennel of house dogs complicates the snow-and-mud problem. We are always resolving to alternate them, two by two, but Melody will look so sad when she goes in the kennel that Jill lets her in, and I am always sneaking out to rescue Little Sister, so that by the time we are ready for bed, Jill says all of a sudden, "I didn't realize we had seven in tonight."

"We didn't have at the beginning," I say. "But honestly, they are so good!"

If I ever built a house, which I am sure is highly unlikely, I would attach the kennel right to it with a nice arched passageway between. Jill says why not just build the kennel large enough for the family to move in there too?

Christmas follows hard on the heels of Thanksgiving. Right after the end of November, the villages get their holiday lights up and string the colored globes over the streets. It is all too sudden and soon for me. It doesn't yet feel like Christmas, and the gifts in the windows seem out of place.

But Mr. Bennet brings Christmas catalogues every day, and Jill begins to ask if I have started the list for the children, and what are we going to give those friends who have everything? I spend a frantic morning hunting last year's list just to be sure we do not send a steak platter to the same cousin we sent one to before.

The catalogues simply fascinate me, especially the ones with fancy food packs and fruits and smoked birds and things shipped in dry ice. I also love the crystal and silver and the velvets and silks—in fact, I seem drawn to almost any kind of gift myself. But fitting the gift to the person is a hazardous job, for all people do *not* like all things.

Christmas giving should be a pleasure, a chance to express to those we love how much they are in our thoughts.

Too often it is just a duty we get involved in, and we are tired and worn out with the whole business of shopping and mailing. But Christmas gifts, when they do have meaning, are a most wonderful expression.

*Where the Mail Comes to Stillmeadow*

Father never had any trouble choosing his gifts for people, he just gave them something he wanted himself. I always remember the year Father gave Mamma the *History of the Cheyenne Indians,* in several volumes. Secretly Mamma had hoped for a new tea set, for every dark cold Wisconsin winter afternoon Mamma made tea and cinnamon toast. And cups did break when I washed!

"Those Indians were wonderful people," Father's blue eyes shone, "you can learn their whole history!"

Mamma did try, up to page eighteen or so, but her heart was never really with the Cheyenne Indians.

My hope that year was for the Little Colonel books. *The Snow Baby,* and *The Roosevelt Bears*—ah, what a book that was!—I knew by heart. Books—I wanted books, books, books, I said.

So Father gave me the complete works of William Shakespeare. Eight volumes. Illustrated.

I fared better than Mamma, for I began with *Romeo and Juliet* and was romantically well nourished until I could cope with *Hamlet.* And years later I read *The Little Colonel* anyway with my own child.

Books were the best gift Santa could bring, and all of my Christmas memories are bound up with books. Other presents were wonderful enough, but that flat rectangular package under the tree—ah, there is the closest thing we know of pure happiness and all tied up in a holly ribbon. A bottle of French scent may be lovely for a time, but all the perfumes of Araby may be between the covers of a book, forever fresh.

Therefore Father's idea of the perfect present was right, as Father always was right, he well knew, even if he invariably gave only the books he himself wanted. He knew what was good and that was what we got, Mamma and I!

We opened our presents Christmas morning, and on Christmas Eve they were piled under the sweet-smelling fir tree Father cut in the swamp and lugged in to town. (He didn't like store trees.)

The smell of mince pies and plum puddings and roasting

turkey drifted through the house. Candles in the windows burned softly to light the Christ Child in, and the carolers came down the snow-deep streets singing *Oh, Little Town of Bethlehem.*

And I would be kneeling to poke those mysterious packages and see how many could conceivably be books—and, oh, if all the aunts and cousins had just *not* picked the same book! One sad year I had fifteen Little Peppers instead of just *Five Little Peppers.*

Maybe there would be a book to carry me to far Cathay, or purple Arabia where the princes ride at noon, or to a green island in a sea of jade—and I could do all this traveling and still stay right at home; I could go across the widest ocean and still be back for supper.

And now, this later Christmas, when countries of the mind invite me as much as the magic countries of childhood, I find I have not changed at all. For I still think that to read is the most exciting of adventures and a pleasure that never ends.

Someday I am even going to go back and read the *History of the Cheyenne Indians!*

By the middle of the month, the house is filled with Christmas. And everything about Christmas is exciting to me. I love the smells—the pine branches we bring in from the woods, snowy and cold, give forth the most heavenly fragrance, and there is the smell of freshly baked Christmas cookies and fruitcake, and a whiff of spring from the apple logs in the fire.

The sounds are fine sounds too. Tissue paper is mysterious when it crisps under the blue and scarlet ribbons; the cracking of nuts has a good sound; even the tinkle of a blue Christmas ball on the floor is a holiday note.

We are never beforehand with the wrapping or the Christmas cards. I did plan to get everything done this year—but so many things keep popping up that here I am in the usual unfinished state. One friend of ours put up a card table in her cellar one steaming August night and addressed all her Christmas cards! Wrote appropriate messages on them too. I admired the feat, but I just never could compose Christmas greetings in the cellar in August.

The color of Christmas is lovely. The deep shining green, and the scarlet and blue, the flame color of the candles in the windows, the rosy glow of the baked ham—there are many enchanting colors. The color of Christmas is dramatic, triumphant.

But the best thing of all is that it is a time of friends remembering one another, families gathering together, a time when people open their hearts. It is a time when one can be sentimental and not hide it.

Perhaps the real significance of Christmas is that we need it so much. Now there are people who say they feel it is purely commercialized, it has lost its real spirit. But this is not so. All the expensive gadgets in the world of shops, if stood in a heap, would not really hide the real spirit of Christmas in the heart of one single buyer who timidly hopes to afford something special for a girl with gray eyes. Anyone who scoffs at Christmas should stand on a snowy evening and look in the faces of the shoppers, tired, maybe, harassed, upset because Aunt Mary just has everything. And there comes that look of love suddenly easing the lines of fatigue when they think of how happy someone will be with something they *did* dream up!

No matter in what state our world is, Christmas comes round again to renew our belief in brotherhood and peace and give us hope.

When I was growing up, we used to pack the gifts in baskets and carry them around the little town late Christmas Eve—meaning between five and seven. How I loved those snowy walks with a basket filled with red and gold and green packages. I always think of it now when most presents mean standing in line at the post office. Mamma used to tie sprigs of holly in the ribbons.

The stars would come out over the church spire, and the sound of carols was in the air, and it was all wonderful and exciting, for there was no dark current of war as yet. Mamma made pounds of Christmas candies, sweet and bitter chocolates, fondant, divinity fudge, panocha, Turkish delight.

Then we had ribbon candy in lurid green and red and blue, and big striped candy canes sharp with peppermint. Oh, yes, stuffed dates, and almonds browned in butter. There were no shortages then, except of oranges and grapefruit. An orange in the toe of the stocking was wonderful.

The cooking for Christmas is fun. Jill and I begin days ahead baking and brewing. We bring the turkey up from the freezer in time to thaw well. We usually stuff our birds

before freezing, and I like chestnut or cornbread stuffing
for the turkey. Our own cranberry sauce is special, because
the wild cranberries in the meadow are large and sweet.

For years we had a frantic hunt every year for Grandma
Raybold's plum-pudding recipe, in her slanting, faded
handwriting on yellowed old letter paper. Now we have
it in the cookbook and turn smartly to the page. Jill says
it is worth all the work of getting the recipes together to
be able to lay our hands on what we want. I sometimes
feel doubtful when I think of how I felt when we found
the cup of applesauce had been left out of the applesauce-
cake recipe by an error. A horrid fear has beset me ever
since that I might go down in history as the woman who
tried to make applesauce cake with no applesauce!

The snow falls so softly, with such tranquil flakes. It is
the quietest thing in all the world, except perhaps the
midnight moon on still summer water. Around Thanksgiving we may get snow, usually a scurry of clouds and
whirling light frothy snow. But the week before Christmas
we begin to see the sky colored like the breast of a sea
gull, and the air has an intensity about it as dark falls
sudden and soon.

Then one day it comes, first one starry flake, then a few
more, and whiteness silently fills the whole air. Now it
is really snowing!

The little towns in the valley are beautiful in the snow.
All the doorways are green with pine; the tall trees in
the center of the village greens are blossoming with colored

lights and red and blue and green balls. The children pull their sleds out, although the grass is hardly covered yet. In their warm peaked caps and bunny suits and fuzzy mittens and boots, they look like children from a German fairy tale. At the post office the villagers gather, the men stamp their galoshes on the stoop and cast an eye at the sky, and wait to hear what Ed Munson says about the weather. Ed has been watching the weather for eighty years, and he knows how long it will snow.

At the grocery store, the farm women have pink cheeks and bright eyes and they are buying red candles and currants and cinnamon drops and the wonderful old-fashioned ribbon candy which is back again. There are boxes of scarlet and yellow lollipops, just the right size to fit an open mouth.

And at the village garage, Arza Bennet is deciding whether or not we need the chains on. With the snow tires, probably not. Even if this turns out to be a three-day snow, he says, the roads will be all right. It's a good snow, no sleet in it.

George is bringing us a big Yule log, and we are frantically hunting for the Christmas tree stand which is always, always missing. How carefully we put away all the ornaments last year, and the lights and that stand! Too carefully, says Jill, brushing cobwebs from her hair as she gets down from the attic.

I like to get the tree up early, for it is so beautiful and the holidays are so short anyway. And if the cut end is placed in water to which half a cupful of blackstrap molasses has been added, the needles keep fresh and stay on the branches a long time.

We planted five hundred Christmas trees a few years ago, on the slope beyond the meadow. But I don't know whether we shall ever cut them, even if they grow big enough in our time. The theory is that you cut them on a planned basis, and they keep on developing. But a whole

*Fifteen Bowls for Christmas Breakfast*

stand of Christmas trees will be so lovely to look at! For after all, no tree can be better decorated than with pure drifts of dazzling snow.

This is the first Christmas for Linda and Flyer's children. Souvenir and Night Flyer Second are wild with excitement at all the crisping of tissue paper and the unrolling of ribbons. What is better to pounce on than a nice shiny Christmas angel? Why don't we do this more often, says Sue, trailing tinsel behind her as she races.

The older dogs and cats are more sedate about it, so

they can give their full attention to the kitchen. Honey begins to wag toward the stove the minute the turkey is brought up from the freezer, and Esmé begins her holiday Siamese wail. There is nothing for it but, as soon as the turkey is half done, a bit has to be sliced off somewhere in an inconspicuous spot for the sapphire-eyed one.

Maeve has all of the Irish setter's traditional eagerness and curiosity. Every time Jill ties a ribbon on a package she nearly ties in a red velvet nose with it. I guess she thinks her name is *Maeve, Stop,* Jill opines.

There is a slight problem with the cat, Sydney, who comes with Dorothy and Val. In summer he can stay in the studio, but in winter he has to be upstairs right where Esmé can sense his alien presence. We are accustomed to sudden bangings as Esmé tries to go right through a locked batten door to get at Sydney. The spirit of hospitality has never, never penetrated our Esmé's heart. She yowls some, too, but Sydney never says anything. I often think, that, like many women, Esmé does not know how silly she is, for Sydney is a very large, very active unpedigreed strong male, and I think he would finish her off in a hurry. Women have a way of assuming they are right, sometimes, just because they can make more racket!

Cicely gets off the train half hidden in luggage. I always know when she is about to descend for at that point the conductor turns around and begins to hand down boxes and bags and parcels and a suitcase the size of a trunk.

"My presents," she says, waving at the mountain of things, "I don't know why they are all funny shapes."

Don, on the other hand, may come back from college without even a clean shirt. He has stopped over in town with Cicely and slipped his gifts in her luggage, and he comes on a later train.

The little old house begins to fill up the week before Christmas. Radios go on in the upstairs bedrooms, the records are playing in the front living room, Val and Don are dealing for Canasta on the trestle table where we really ought to have lunch. The girls want more paper and more tags, and we are always out of tags.

Jill is trying to find out which light is dead on the tree string. I am basting the turkey, stepping out and around a bevy of cockers, and wondering whether the plum pudding is done.

Our present to Stillmeadow this year was an electric dishwasher. This is one gadget we thought never to succumb to. We said you had to rinse the dishes anyway and stack them, and why not finish them off the way our mothers and grandmothers have been doing for generations?

But all summer we were cooking and washing for as many as eight or nine at a time, and no help, of course. And there was always the question, Who is going to wash the dishes this time? When the children are home, we like to go to the movies in the next town, and that means booting out at six forty—dishes waiting until we get back.

We hadn't expected to use it unless we had company, but we discovered at once that you can stack all the dishes for a whole day in it, turn it on after dinner at night, and never wipe a thing. It releases a lot of time for things like brushing the dogs, or canning the mushrooms George brings over, or polishing the toaster and broiler. And the glasses shine better, the plates are clean front and back —and where is the good housewife who doesn't do over a few plates washed by guests and/or children?

Also, which is a fine feature, dishes for a person with a cold come out germ-free. It is a job to keep a tray load of separate dishes for one sneezer and sniffler.

Incidentally, I have long believed that one good house present is a fine thing for any family to give at Christmas. We always give Stillmeadow—and nice for us who live in it—a present. In lean years it might be a heat-proof platter or a new frying pan—spider to us New Englanders. In particularly good years, it has been an antique table or a comb-back chair. But the idea is that it should be something that every soul who enters the house should enjoy. Something to make life more amiable. I think this is an idea all families might well adopt.

I know some men who feel that anything for the house is especially for the women. But it isn't. Even new curtains that make the living room a gay place are really for the whole family and add to the pleasure in the home. Even the husband who drops ashes on the rug is really happier dropping them on a rug that is a new fresh color!

And dishes are a lot of work, for so many people. Besides, we have had our main family conflict, the one unresolvable one, about dishes. The children like to *leave them* for hours, while they do other things. They like, all of them, to Let Their Dinner Digest.

Jill and I like to get them out of the way *immediately,* and not have them to anticipate, getting worse by the minute.

"If you'll just wait, Mamma," Cicely wails, "we'll do them. But we want to play the new Piaf records first."

So usually Jill and I keep sneaking a few out, and rinsing them, and just doing the glasses. And then the children rush out and revile us. We were brought up to get hard things done as fast as possible, and their generation was brought up to ease along with life.

I was thinking about all of this when I went to visit the Shentons in their lovely old stone house in the Pennsylvania hills. They had a dishwasher *and* a maid, which seemed too elegant for words. But the maid had to go home after dinner to West Chester, and I was worried about how late that must be. There were ten for dinner that first night, a wonderful and very dish-consuming kind of dinner. And we were just sitting around the fire drinking our after-dinner coffee when the maid appeared in the door, hatted and gloved and ready to go home! The dishwasher was turned on, and the kitchen was as clean as a new penny, and in the morning she would unload the racks—and there it was, just like saying *abracadabra.*

"I am sold," I said, "I am really sold on this thing."

If there is one thing that is characteristic of Americans, about whom one can say a lot of adverse things, it is that we are a nation of home folks. And I think we shall always be so. From a flat over a drugstore to a penthouse over New York, home is the real focus of our living. Perhaps this will save America in the end.

We do live in parlous times. Nobody can deny it. With the divorce rate skyrocketing, and foreign troubles sitting like gray wolves outside the door, and politics a shambles, and unrest in every industry, and the economic situation unstable, we know that life is grave. Our country is full of underprivileged people; we face crises not once a month but every week. I know all this. I know we are bigoted and narrow—and I read many letters from women who say they will not bring a child into this world because they are afraid.

But oh, as Christmas comes again, I know an inner security about life that I wish I could share. The old tired earth is most beautiful and lovely. As long as men come home from work and children from school and women put a sprig of parsley on the platter so the steak or the chicken or the spaghetti may look festive, so long as the church bells ring in the frosty air, we have a world worth living for.

And Christmas is the time when we can understand this, even if we are sad or lonely or in trouble as so many people are on this scrap of whirling matter-in-space. For this is the season of living as deeply as we may, of loving, and of the expression of the values of life that we believe in.

From the smallest little card which says Merry Christmas to the most expensive present that can be bought, the meaning of Christmas comes to us all. And the greatest gifts are the intangible ones, purchased by the spirit and not by coins.

These we may freely spend and have no budget. They may be the thoughtful errand the neighbor runs, or the driveway shoveled out by a friend. Or letters of friendship. A bit of sewing for someone who cannot run up a dish towel. Any loving deed or word, this is the magic of Christmas!

On Christmas Eve we light the candles in the windows to light the Christ Child in, and this is a testament of faith. I always hope the real spirit of the Christ Child will burn in our hearts as clearly as the pointed candle flame. And although I love the new elegant candles—the little winged angels and cherubs and the big twisted heavy red and blues and whites—I am always mindful that it is the flame that matters.

The tree, too, is a symbol. How good the scent of pine, how bright the fragile gold and blue glass balls, how shining the tinsel and the delicate glass icicles! But this tree, this year, as the tree my mother used to trim on long-ago Christmas Eves, has a meaning beyond any individual tree. It is a symbol of the rich growth which Nature gives us all—out of the dark and frozen earth under the snow came the seed, comes the lifting spire of green. Unless we destroy her, the earth will grow green in spring, bear in summer, glow in autumn, and dream in winter. The seasons with their infinite splendor will roll on; the glory of the sun and moon will be vouchsafed to us. This is the promise of my Christmas tree.

George has managed the Yule log, just big enough to make the old hearth bulge. He made a wreath last year for his own house door, with the help of a carpenter named Olsen, and it was lovelier than any I saw made by the garden-club members. It was shaded green with different evergreens and woven intricately with bunches of bright red berries.

When the moon comes up over the snow on Christmas Eve, I think the world was never so beautiful. The yard is ribboned with long delft-blue shadows and patterned by flying cocker paws. The house has every window lighted extravagantly—for Christmas comes but once a year.

And the sound of the best of carols lifts the heart again:

> "God rest you merry, gentlemen,
> Let nothing you dismay——"

Pile high the hickory and the light
Log of chestnut struck by the blight.
Welcome-in the winter night.

Here are question and reply,
And the fire reflected in the thinking eye.
So peace, and let the bob-cat cry.

Edna St. Vincent Millay

## CHAPTER TEN

It takes an open mind and a ready heart to appreciate winter in New England. The wind blows, the snow piles deep, the car gets stuck, and pipes freeze. It is easy to dream of the South Sea islands, with coral beaches and sapphire water and strange tropical fruit dropping in your hand.

But under the hard and bitter rind of winter, there is much loveliness. The white mystery of snow is a splendid thing; all the landscape is muted to deep silver laced with blue shadows. The meadow is a sea of pearl with scattered dark masts of brier riding the foam. The cool, clean smell of snow is in the air, a special fragrance known only to winter country.

The sounds are fine too. The ring of skates on black ice on the pond, and the laughter of children making snow men, and the soft thud of hoofs as the horses stamp in the barn on a frosty morning. The crackle of apple wood in the fireplace.

January is drama in the season. Driving against the pane comes the sleet, and wild is the sound of the wind from the fierce heart of winter. The sky can be black as anthracite, and the drifts roll under it.

In the house, there is a special sense of security. The house is as tight and snug as a ship. In the old black kettle swinging from the crane, Cranberry Island stew is simmering. The range glows in the back kitchen, and beans are baking for Saturday-night supper. A few cockers are dripping on the hearth, and the cats are asleep on the hottest radiator.

Dark comes down early, and in the country we eat supper by the time the night settles in, which means we are through early and have some time to read. The books we never got around to in summer come into their own. I finally read Stendhal's *le Rouge et le Noir,* which gives such a picture of a different period and different emotions that it is like a journey to a new land.

And all those vegetables and fruits we put down in the heat of summer in the freezer come out now, like new-picked treasures. Asparagus and sweet corn and the glowing ruby-red raspberries and strawberries taste like summer herself.

We refinish a piece of old furniture at leisure, or paint a little woodwork. Someone told us about the trick of setting the paint can on a paper plate. The drippings soon make the plate stick firmly and no paint is spilled, and there is a place to put the brush down.

We try to get the cleaning equipment in order. Oil mops

we let stand an hour or so in a pail which has a gallon of hot soapsuds and three tablespoons of turpentine in it. Then we wash and dry the mop, and reoil it. Brooms and whisk brooms benefit by a dipping in water and a good shaking.

I like pancakes for breakfast, with our own maple sirup. For extra-fine ones, I separate the eggs and add the beaten whites last. And leftover pancake batter is no loss, for we put it in the refrigerator and use it at noon or night for batter. Dipping slices of pineapple in it and deep-frying them gives delicate fritters and means no waste.

We ration our sirup, for probably we never shall have another bout with our own trees; staying up all night to empty the pails was an adventure once, but a little too hard to become routine. Besides, the steam took all the paint off the kitchen ceiling. But the sirup is delicious. A very light color and sweeter than a dream. Incidentally, apples baked with maple sirup are elegant.

In Revolutionary times, fresh meat was supposed to be unhealthy, salted meat being good. Potatoes were deadly if eaten more than once a week in the Colonial days. To-matoes—they were suspect. And people boiled everything to death. They had never heard of vitamins. Now we are practically enslaved by them.

But some of the early meals were magnificent. For in-stance, in Boston, around 1860, breakfast could be stewed pigeons with mushrooms, deviled gizzards, liver pudding, pork cheese, hashed poultry, minced veal, and five other things including sausage and fish cakes and broiled tomatoes. A nice start for the day! When I read the old menus and look at the wasp-waisted slim ladies in the pictures, I can't help feeling something is wrong somewhere. Did they eat all of those dishes, or did they nibble slightly, or how in the world did they, if plump, get laced in to those tiny dimensions? In any case, those elegant, fabulous menus would put any modern woman into a stupor just to contemplate.

In winter, the Obedience Club meets indoors in a town which is supposed to be a central meeting place. On hot summer nights it is easy to drive halfway up or down Connecticut, but how the distances do lengthen out in the big snows! However, where dogs are concerned, human beings develop marvelous powers of endurance and stability.

Nobody wants to cut class, for there is always a show coming up, and maybe Bing will refuse the jumps or Sister miss her dumbbell retrieve if she lacks practice.

The Long Down is usually the downfall of our cockers. The dogs are lined up and told to "Down—Stay," and then the handlers walk away—and walk right on out of sight, if it is the advanced class. For five minutes the dogs are supposed to remain motionless while the handlers hide. The longest five minutes on record this time is, and when the call comes, "Handlers, return to your dogs," it is a sound of pure bliss.

But the cockers have trouble. They lie down amiably

while you are there, and then as you walk nervously across
the floor they begin to creep forward, paw by anxious
paw. You go back and get them down again. You scurry
away. They scurry too. You say "Shame," rather feebly.
For after all, it is flattering to be so important that your
dog cannot bear to be away from you for even five minutes!

Sometimes, if the snow is not too deep, we go to class
in Bristol. It takes about forty-five minutes to get there,
and the drive is beautiful in the cold pure moonlight. The
villages are lighted and the woods have a pale glow from
the snow. The hills and valleys have such an untouched
look.

The class meets in the armory, and half of the floor is
given to the dog training while in the other half a group
of young boys drill with a smart sergeant to call the army
commands. The noise is earsplitting, but everybody gets
used to it. I am fascinated by the sight of the two kinds
of discipline being practiced at once. The recruits get into
trouble with their marching; the dogs get too wide on
their own about-turns. It seems peculiarly American to
me to combine army drill with dog training. A single narrow bench down the middle of the floor separates the two
groups, and it is sufficient.

I may say that the dogs seem to learn faster.

The faces of the boys are so smooth and young. The
drill is good for the slim bodies, color rises in the un-
shadowed cheeks, now and then a faint giggle cannot be
repressed when one boy starts marching off all alone in

the wrong direction. It is all such a fine thing—provided it is only for discipline and exercise and not with the idea of a new war in mind.

For the dog people the objective is a sound one, no doubt about it. The dogs are better citizens, and so are the handlers. The shows take the place of examinations in school; they are not the real end and aim, although how wonderful it is when your own little problem child brings in a blue ribbon or a piece of silver!

Now we have nine degrees at Stillmeadow, and we have the glorious memory of Little Sister going Best Obedience dog at Meadowbrook and winning a nice large silver loving cup. A lot of things are in that cup, long hours of work, hot suns and cold winds, moments of discouragement and moments of pride. The failures are there when Sister got timid at a show and blew up completely. The successes are there too, when she surmounted her natural shyness and jumped with precision even when small boys swung on the ropes beside her.

But mainly, to me, it is a symbol of the working companionship that Little Sister and I established. Her timidity and my arthritis in the end gave in to our efforts.

The cockers are easier to train than Maeve. The Irish-setter temperament does not go with any activity which is not self-inspired. Heeling bores Maeve stiff. She has an elfish sense of humor too, and may decide in the show ring to nip Jill gayly as she makes the rightabout turn. Or she may bound up suddenly and embrace the judge, just as a sign that there are no hard feelings anywhere.

She learns like lightning, but perhaps she does not feel like sitting this time. She has to be in the mood.

Maeve won her CDX in three straight shows, but there was a decided look of surprise on Jill's face each time when Maeve steadied herself down and minded her business.

Obedience work is a fine opportunity to study human beings as well as dogs. Miss X thinks her dog is stubborn and never wonders whether she herself is making her wants clear. I know that at home nothing is ever her fault, she is always put upon by others. One handler always blames the judge if his dog fails. Other people must have pull, he thinks, to get a good score.

Then there are people like Danny Peters who went to show after show with his Doberman, Lance. Lance was a perfect performer in every exercise right up to the very last one, the Utility Stand for examination. When that began, Lance just trotted out of the ring.

Danny would reach over and snap her leash on, and smile, and walk away. He always said, "One day there will come a time when she will stand." The next show, it would go on all over again.

And one day she did stand. Patience and practice won out, and Danny moved proudly up to take his prize for a top-working dog. A top-working man, too, I thought, as he bent over to pat Lance proudly.

There is one match show in autumn that I especially like, for this show has the blessing of the dogs. St. Hubert is the patron saint of dogs, and at this show all the dogs and their handlers receive the blessing of St. Hubert.

In the middle of the show, the loud-speaker gives the order. All judges stop judging when the time is called, and the priest mounts a green decorated platform with autumn leaves banked above it. The handlers and the dogs stand in a ring below, and the audience makes a larger circle outside.

The blessing is preceded by a small speech about the value of dog's and man's companionship down the ages, and then the Latin phrases sound out in the still cool air.

I like this, I like everything about it. It is good that in the midst of a day of sport and competition, men will stop for such a thing. And it is good that Methodist dogs like my own may have the same blessing pronounced over them; it is a small moment in time when one catches a glimpse of what the world would be like if there were unity between all religions. The main thing is that we be blessed, each according to his need, and ah, if only we could always remember that!

Maybe it is easier for dog people to develop tolerance. The Catholic collie that takes the jumps never has a Protestant poodle looking down his muzzle at him. It is what they do that is noticed. How they behave.

Coming home from a winter show, we are tired and hungry. In summer I begin to long for iced tea the minute we check out of the gate; in winter I anticipate boiling Darjeeling. And a good hearty supper eaten in front of an apple-wood fire.

How good a hot plate feels to numb fingers! But the

dogs come first—they get their dinner as soon as our mittens are off and wraps hung up.

One of the by-products of following the circuit in dog shows is the camaraderie which develops among the dog people. I fancy it is a lot like circus performers. The smell of the sawdust cannot be more exciting than the sign on the first telephone pole pointing the way. *Dog show*, it says, and a red arrow points down some winding road.

Once there, the handlers converge on the ring. Everyone tells everyone else just how badly or wonderfully his or her dog did yesterday or last week in class. But don't expect anything now. I never yet met a handler whose dog was not letter perfect at home. The fabulous performances of dogs at home is something amazing! At least, that is the story.

Amateurs have a way of explaining this to the judge, who only looks bored. He has heard this too often. If he is a good judge, he stands and waits until the tale is told; if he is not a good judge, he snaps the handler into the exercise with a cold word.

There have been a number of articles lately on the necessity of developing hobbies and outside interests to prevent a kind of mental dry rot setting in. But dog people never have time to think of themselves or how they feel, they are entirely occupied with the present state of their dogs!

And as they trail away from one show, there is always the next one to look forward to where conditions will be Elysian and the dogs will all win ribbons!

One boiling day our trainers, Ardella and Hazel, plus

Ardella's sister and Hazel's daughter and four cockers and one enormous Great Pyrenees were all ensconced in a small coupé sweating their way to a show. They passed a golf course and saw two men broiling on the fairway.

"I wonder what ever makes people spend their time like that?" said Hazel dreamily.

Ardella laughed. "Maybe they wonder about us!" she said, pushing a cocker off her neck.

On class nights, all the cockers who are in training or have ever been in training begin to leap about and bark excitedly and trip us up and generally raise Ned. They try to get us off beginning with six o'clock, and all the time we eat supper they bound around, saying, Hurry up, time to go! Let's get off!

Since no handler can train more than one dog at a time, we only take *three* each time, and getting away from the ones elected to keep the home fires burning is a dreadful ordeal. The languishing looks, the sobs we leave behind are tragic. They all want to go. The minute Jill picks up a training collar, the house is full of necks stretched out for it.

And we work hard all evening. After two hours of running around a gym, everybody is worn out. When the trainer says, "Drop your dog!" I can hear a voice say, "I should think you'd be *glad* to lie down—I would!" as the handler leans on a fifty-five pound mass of resisting dog flesh.

We chose Melody as our first dog to train because, as Jill said, "If she can learn, anybody can!"

Melody is erratic, stubborn as a pair of mules, charming, dreamy, high-strung, temperamental as an opera singer. Ravishing, but never stable. She was a war casualty, too, for during the war nobody came to the place, and when life resumed its usual tenor Melody was timid. When called she crept under the range, and when visitors came she flew out of sight.

It took six weeks to teach her to sit. But after a time, she did get the willingness to do what she should, and now there isn't a merrier, friendlier, better behaved dog on the place, and as for company, she has her paw out in welcome to everyone who steps in the gate!

She comes when she is called, even though she knows it means going to the kennel for her turn. We used to have to chase her half an hour to get her in.

Now that we have those nine degrees, the two puppies are just about the right age to start kindergarten! So we begin all over again!

And what do we do in our spare time? Go out in the back yard and work a couple of dogs retrieving dumbbells over the high jump.

We are reliving the adventures of beginning life in the country in the experiences of our young neighbors, Ruth and Eddie, who moved into a little house on the hill last August. Having lived in a city apartment all their lives, they were afraid they might be lonesome. Now they wonder how they ever stood it in the city where there is nothing to do and it is lonesome! In the city, the man who put in new bathroom tiles would never have given them a Persian painting he collected while a G.I. Nor would the carpenter have settled comfortably with a cool drink and told long tall tales of life in the early days. And the postman would not stop for a chat about planting Chinese chestnuts for the birds. The discovery of people is one of the first surprises to country neophytes. And then Eddie discovered the sky.

"Every morning when I wake up and look out," he said breathlessly, "there is the sky—all over everything. I never dreamed it would be like that."

And Ruth found out that broccoli grows on tall plants above ground, not in bunches in the vegetable stall. And that you dig parsnips after frost. When they had their first fresh-picked zucchini, gardeners were born. A whole new intricate fascinating world of growing things opened up.

Then there are all those other things that happen. After two baths, of course, the well went dry. The pressure tank was unbalanced, and air blew violently from the pipes. The carpenter cut down too many trees while they were away one day. Wasps and hornets staged family reunions all over the little house. The foundation turned out to be entirely fictional and the whole house had to be "yacked up," as Mr. Olsen said, and refounded on good stone.

Fifteen years of country dwelling have not taken the savor from the spring music of the peepers, and thinking it over as Ruth and Eddie start the same way of life, it seems to me a whole lifetime is not long enough to make the delicate excitements of spring less wonderful, nor the deep richness of summer, nor the blazing splendor of autumn, nor the pure austerity of winter.

For instance, it was only last autumn that I met the fox. He was leaping across the tawny field, his brush a burnished color, his pointed face silhouetted against gray stone. I walked slowly toward him and he turned and looked at me, and most incredibly started toward me. A cynic would say he knew I had no long pointed thing in my arms raised to send thundering death into him, but I fondly thought he knew instinctively that I was merely another living being. The woods and fields were deep with sunlight, and the lovely color of the sky was like pale silk over us. It was an enchanted moment for us both. He gave a graceful pirouette, and then reason and common sense took over, and he flirted his brush and leaped back into the shelter of the thicket.

Now a new year begins, and we can take out the resolutions we made last year and didn't keep, polish them up, and try again. But after all, the only resolution we really need is to work for real peace among all the nations. And no one is too obscure to help, for it is really the sum of the people that moves the government. And if every voice in America says, "There shall be no war," the volume of sound will become thunder in the ears.

On a January night in our snowy valley, it is easy to

have faith. It is so still and the snow is falling so quietly. The village church spire lifts a silvery tip, and the little white houses glow with the warm supper lights. The lights of Stillmeadow shine on our own drifts.

And Honey moves like a pale gold shadow on the terrace, sniffing with delight the fresh pure air of a new year!

The Valley in the Snow

New England cooking is the thing for deep winter. The kind of food our forefathers invented out of the simple fare the rock-bound coast afforded was hearty and comforting. It still is.

Take beans, for instance, and molasses and salt pork, and you get those big brown crocks bubbling over with crusty brown goodness for Saturday night.

The Indians taught the early settlers the uses of maize, but it took the pioneer women to make Indian pudding, corncake, muffins, crackling bread, and my favorite, Spider Corn Bread.

Here in the country we greet the New Year without any wild celebrations. I think it is because we are attuned to the changing seasons, and in the midst of winter we are looking to spring. So we never get that curious panic that time has gone by and we should drown our old year out and racket the new in. George comes over on one morning and says, "Happy New Year," and goes out to shovel his way to the kennel. We plow about gathering eggs warm and new. Maeve whisks her tail in the drifts. The house smells sweet with the holiday greens and the big country ham a-baking. Jill gets up more of our own wild-cranberry sauce. I put the fat acorn squash in to bake.

The children are home. It is all so much, suddenly, as it used to be when they were not grown and leading their own lives, that I feel I could wake up and find myself back in time.

It seems even more likely when they haul out the old sled and go off to slide down the snowy hill. Dorothy and Val have been married going on three years, but they look like children in their woolly ski suits and big flapping mittens.

In winter, the fire on the hearth is the center of the life at Stillmeadow. In summer, life flows outward. Someone is in the barbecue typing, someone else is in the Quiet Garden reading *Tales of the South Pacific* or *Running of the Tide*. The girls are out in their own summerhouse; Don and Val, with the new gun, are blasting away at a tomato can nailed to an old apple tree. Someone else is up in the studio, and Jill is down the meadow with Maeve "seeking back" an old glove. I, of course, am in the kitchen.

Sometimes our casual spreading around causes trouble. There was the day last August when our friend Johannes got locked in the studio. The studio is the old haymow, and the old double doors have a way of swinging back in a breeze and locking. Johannes went up to Be Alone and finish his book, and alone he really was, for the doors swung back and when he tried to come out, he found he was tightly shut up.

At first he was not worried. He leaned out the window and called mildly. Nobody paid the least attention except a couple of spaniels who were after squirrels below. They barked loudly. He raised his voice. So did they. The kennel took it up and a thunderous racket ensued, with Johannes yelling. Then he worked at the door, the nice heavy old chestnut door. Nothing gave except Johannes. So he went back and called again. But he had asked for an uninterrupted time to work and he got it.

Finally it came to him that not even for lunch would the family interrupt art. Who would intrude on a love scene with crab salad? He had a new idea. Being a Viennese, he is a fine yodeler. Or perhaps not all Viennese can yodel, but he is our only friend who can. So he yodeled. He yodeled with the very best yodel.

But the cockers had never heard anybody yodel before, and when they heard that sound from up above, they made noise enough to drown a bombing attack. They went really wild. Yodeling and barking went on for as long as Johannes could breathe, and then he gave up and resigned himself to a life in the studio, starving and helpless but with his manuscript beside him. He mopped his brow and eventually located a coat hanger. This he wrenched into a kind of bar, with which he managed to pick the latch and escape.

We were serenely stringing beans for the freezer when he appeared. I thought he must have been working very hard, he looked so hot and tired.

Jill looked up. "I hope the dogs didn't bother you," she said. "For some reason, they have been making an awful racket this morning."

The color of winter is pure and lovely, the long, darkly blue shadows, the purple stalks of the briery bushes, the glistening white of clean snow, the pale amber of shell ice where the little brooks walk in summer. The meadow is latticed now with the pattern of dark branches and the great timeless trees lift intricate patterns against a still sky.

Yes, lovely is this world of ours, I think, as I look up at the pearl-clear light over the snowy valley. Surely all we need for the new year is peace over the world so men can lift their eyes to the sky and know that death will not hover over.

Honey pads along with her own thoughts, which have rabbits in them, and all her yesterdays, and being a loved companion, and the memory of tonight's snack, and maybe an idea as to tomorrow's leftover waffle with a smidgen of wild-flower honey on it. For she has reached the age when she can have just about anything she wants and no nonsense about it.

As I turn back toward the little white house on New Year's evening, I wish with all my heart that the serenity of woods and hills and valleys could be shared with the whole restless and uneasy world.

"Happy New Year," I say softly, and the wind in the leafless hazel bush picks up my words and carries them on, far away, toward tomorrow!

## CHAPTER ELEVEN

Come now the wild dark days of February when the house seems like a lovely warm little island with winter billowing outside. Pipes freeze and get thawed out, and there is a sense of victory. The current goes off, and we move dinner hastily to the coal range or hang it over the fireplace in the old black kettle.

We used to be timid about going out when the storm was bad, but years have seasoned our spirits. We bundle up, put a pail of sand and a shovel in the car, and sally forth. Jill says when we have to make concessions to the weather, we shall be old. So last week end we went right on to Fay and Andy's in Middlebury, in a black, bleak storm. I admit that I liked the drifted road with the car lights turning the snowbanks to crystal. And the desolate waste of the fields was dramatic under the heavy sky. Every tree was a lithograph in black and white.

The current was off at Sleepy Hollow, but Fay had the house lighted with plenty of candles, and they sent a soft warm glow across the snow. All the fireplaces had good sturdy fires in them, and the range looked as comfortable as a summer day. Half a dozen friends came in, stamping the snow from their galoshes, and the roast beef came from the oven sizzling with juices. Fay's creamed potatoes went with it—my favorite. And a chef's salad, and hot mince pie and coffee. Good fare for a winter night.

How much art there can be, I thought that evening, in all the small ways of living. Sometimes we get lazy, but I think the effort spent in putting an ironstone bowl of pine branches on the table is well spent. And getting out the fragile grandmother china is worth it too. Often we do not bother to use the small gracious touches, and it is a pity. For no matter what heaven may be like, there is no use just waiting for it. I'll take mine now, with an open fire and apples toasting on a stick and good friends gathered around the hearth. Bowls of popcorn, and nuts to crack while the talk is merry.

Another recent expedition was made to the Goldmans', where I saw the first really fine collection of dolls I ever beheld. It was like history in miniature, for the dolls reflect the whole life of the time. I have seldom felt more moved than when Emma lifted out a doll made in 1710. It was a small doll, with a wooden body, but with jointed arms and legs, patiently carved out and fitted by hand.

Her face was delicately shaped, and must have looked like the little girl who owned her, rather solemn and grave. Time had worn away some of her frock and bonnet, but enough was left of the faded blue and the lacy edging. I thought of that long-ago little girl who loved this doll, played with her, and was careful with her—so careful the doll is still perfect.

All the stories her doll might tell are packed away in the silk-lined box. But I thought her meaning was plain: that children, even in the shadow of war, build a make-believe world of their own—a world where their dolls are safe and the sun is shining.

I shall never be able to have a wonderful doll collection, but it is a fine thing to preserve and pass on the dolls of the past. And the dolls in native costumes are worth handing down, too, for there may well be a day when native costumes are gone. As countries get divided up and passed around, as people fly all over the world, probably everyone will dress alike, more's the pity.

Some of the period dolls were surprising, for they looked like modern fashion plates. And while I love the old things, and the quaintness of the past, I myself shall never be pinched in at the waist and padded out with a bustle. I am greatly disillusioned by the current victory of the designers over women. I have a fatal tendency to speculate, when I see one of those vast sweeping skirts, on how many small starving children could be dressed in the excess material. I dare say they wouldn't be, but why not?

Banquets are the same kind of flaunting of riches over need. Suppose every banquet for a year were merely a normal meal and all the extra courses were packed in boxes and shipped abroad? How much food would we send?

Here in the country, we feel easier about food when we

raise every bit we can, and when we freeze or put up the whole year's supplies. We may not quite see how that extra row of carrots which we do not buy is going to get to Europe, but we feel it is helping somehow.

Linda and Little Sister have been staying in the house for a week, and so has Hildegarde. Melody and Honey are always in, so there have been five cockers around the fire. Quite a bevy. Melody is a window-sill dog and leaps on my sill beside the milk-glass butter dish. Little Sister is too plump to make it, but she flings herself up and falls back, and then looks large-eyed at the one who can reach the heights. Linda is the charm girl—wants to be carried and admired extravagantly. Little Sister is brisk and full of projects such as eating the edge off the Oriental rug.

Being litter sisters and raised to a hair's breadth alike, they refute any theory that heredity does not count. For Linda, the black one, "takes after" the black side of the family, and Little Sister, the black and white, takes after the parti-color. It is amazing and fascinating to see the personality difference. Linda is always in trouble. If a ladder fell, it would certainly fall on Linda. If an older dog gets irritated by the high jinks going on and takes a nip, it is Linda that gets nipped. And if anything at all goes wrong, Linda's scream is the loudest scream in the country.

Esmé is very jealous. When they are in, she drapes herself on my neck half the time, complaining in her sharpest Siamese. They make her nervous, she says, because you never know where they will bounce next. She likes to reach from behind the door and slap them, just to see what they will say. Of course it is always Linda that is on the business end of the slap.

Tigger always gets his own way, but he is more polite about it than Esmé. When he wants something, he suggests in a soft voice that it would make you happy to give it to him. If ignored, he just sits and looks steadily at you. Next he rubs against you gently, but firmly. Finally he utters a faint cry indicating that life is ebbing from his sturdy frame by the moment. Then he gets it.

In February, after a big storm, the sun comes out with more brightness than at any other time in the year. The winter sky is pale and far away and the snow is the essence of all the white there is. The glory of the sun, with the pale sky and the white snow, is breath-taking. The light has a purity, a dazzling serenity. I like to go out then, and walk up to the mailbox. How beautiful is the world! How fortunate we are, in spite of everything, to feel the infinite splendor of a day after storm!

The most beautiful snowstorm is the one that comes when the air is relatively mild and the big wet flakes cling to every twig and branch. The trees change to silver and the fields are a soft white sea.

And the gift of quietness is given, for there is no stillness so pure and deep as the stillness of snow. Sounds sink without a ripple in that silence. When Honey and I walk up for the mail, our footfalls are soundless, for only hard snow squeaks.

Honey is a pale gold blur when she runs ahead, and the

mailbox is invisible. On my boots the snow falls in a million intricate crystal shapes. It is always a wonder to look at them and mark the infinite splendor of a world where even a snowflake is fashioned with such perfection.

Day after day the snow piles up, and the dogs bring considerable amounts into the house. It keeps Honey busy washing her paws. Tigger, the black cat, comes in sparkling with white star shapes. The Siamese Esmé has no trouble; she stays on the warm stones of the hearth. Esmé thinks nothing at all of winter; her sapphire eyes are filled with tropical dreams as the snow comes down.

The hens have stopped laying and George brings in just one warm brown egg a day. They go on eating their heads off and chattering and throwing their oystershell around. With chicken feed the price it is, those hens are in the class of women with diamond bracelets.

A fox got in George's henhouse and disposed of three hens the other night. And then Shep, the sagacious farm shepherd, got that fox and treed him and when George came out to shoot him, the shot missed and the fox came down and Shep killed him.

I wish I were more reasonable about such things. I simply cannot help being the fox, although of course I can be the hen too. Also, with no trouble at all, I can be in Shep's paws and know the lovely feeling of saving my master's flock. We have had so many foxes this year that there is a bounty on them, and Shep has earned his keep, which is a fine thing.

But I saw a gray fox leaping over the meadow and

jumping the stone wall, and his movement was poetry. His brush was like a banner against the snow and his pointed face was wild and beautiful. I came home quietly and said never a word; I was not going to betray his free

The Gray Fox

heart, although I felt guilty when I closed the henhouse door extra tight and admonished the cheerful silly hens to stay where they belonged.

There is a nice overstuffed rabbit who lives under the girls' summerhouse, and he comes out to inspect the bird food under the tall maple. A hen pheasant comes there too. Linda and Little Sister come out after their own breakfast and go whooping after the rabbit. He takes a last bite of whatever he has enjoyed and lopes back under the house without much ado. They circle and rush about and feel very pleased with themselves. When they forget him, he hops back out. He looks like a Dürer rabbit—that lovely fawn color and soft long ears.

The hen pheasant is interesting too. Maeve goes wild when she sees that plump form in with the lesser birds. She points, holding her red plume stiff behind her, and she points for quite a while. If she forgets herself and rushes, the pheasant sails up and over the fence into the Quiet Garden and settles down on the snow there. Maeve is not allowed in there, and she never jumps in, but how does the pheasant know that?

Winter is never dull in the country, there is so much to see and so much to learn. It is true that the more sensible birds have gone to soak up the tropic sunshine, but the ones that remain we really get acquainted with. They gather early in the morning, and late in the afternoon. We can watch them while we have breakfast and again when we have our tea and cinnamon toast. I think I like the chickadees best, they are so brisk and gay.

When it is really too cold to go out except to fill the heaters in the kennel, we do a lot of extra household tasks. It is a good time to clean desk drawers, dust the books, wash the milk glass, polish the silver. There are some magical new cleaners and polishers on the market that make housework exciting. There is a furniture polish that leaves a faint minty odor which I love. And a liquid cleaner that will do anything except brush your teeth—and might do that, too, if anyone tried it. Windows, silver, brass, the stove, the refrigerator—it makes them shine. Used on antique plates, it leaves them smooth as silk.

Jill went up in the attic and routed out some old gilt Victorian picture frames and gave them three coats of flat white and framed some of our favorite pictures in them. They look lovely. Now I have become so addicted to white paint that I look at everything from old iron candlesticks to Victorian commodes and wonder whether a coat of nice white paint wouldn't—

The use of white is always a help. It brings out the color of a room, adds charm. Nearly any room, I think, is improved with a little use of frost-white.

There is nothing like a little change in a house in the dead of winter to make the family cheerful. New draperies give a lift to the shabby living room. Or a fresh slip cover with flowers blooming on it. Or a piece of furniture you have wanted for a long time.

One of my recent ideas wasn't so much of a success. I decided there should be a new fixture in the small dressing room upstairs. There was a ceiling light with one large bulb. So we bought a very pretty little ceiling fixture. Jill said she would put it up in just a few minutes. She went down cellar and cut off the house current, also cutting off my oven with the meat roasting in it. Then she went up and took down the old fixture. The new one had no screws. So she came down and descended to the cellar and put on the current so my roast started again. She drove to the village and got more screws and came back, cut off the current, went up and found the new screws were too long.

"I'll have to go back," she said grimly.

"Well, put the electricity on again," I said.

She came back with more screws half an hour later. She had to go to the next village for the right size. By now our neighbor Eddie appeared and went up with her, after the current was cut off, and hammered for an hour.

Later, when the fixture was established on the ceiling, Eddie said, "I can't see where this turns on!"

Jill looked. It was a pretty fixture all right, but it had to be turned on from a wall switch and we had no wall switch. So either we had to leave the light on all the time, or not have it on at all.

So Jill went down cellar and cut off the current again and they took off the new fixture. To date, we have no light at all now in that dressing room, and I am regretting my nice idea. At least the bulb did go on when you pulled a string!

Valentine's Day is upon us, almost my favorite of the holidays, for it is romantic and gay—and sentimental. It is a holiday for the young, but it may be the heart is young no matter what the birthday book says. I love valentines, but not funny ones. I do not think jokes belong to the day at all. It is a time for hearts and roses and little birds with sweet messages in their bills. Laces and ribbons belong to it, and the scent of old-fashioned lavender or white lilac.

It is a time to remember the people we love, and a time

to eat happily of bonbons and coconut creams and never mind the calories. Not that candy is the food of love the rest of the year at all! But it reminds me of the colored boxes tied with improbably purple ribbons that the first beau carries so proudly to his girl.

When I was growing up, a copy of the *Rubáiyát* bound in leather was a favorite gift. I had quite a lot of copies. It is surprising that the *Rubáiyát* was so correct, for if I reread it now, I can see the message is not just what most parents would have approved of. Certainly turning down an empty glass was not my father's idea under any circumstances. Boiled down, that poem simply says have all the pleasure you can for there will be no tomorrow. Possibly, if the atom-bomb specialists have their way, we had better begin to follow the *Rubáiyát* right now!

It is particularly nice to have Valentine's Day fall in the depths of winter, for it suggests that spring is really just around the corner.

The seed catalogues are a further promise of warm days to come. I class them as fiction and love to read them. Oh, the beautiful roses and tall spikes of delphinium and the flowering bushes—not to mention the carrots as big as telephone poles and the peas that practically shell themselves and hop with a mint leaf into boiling water. We get some pretty fine vegetables and some nice flowers, but they definitely do not resemble the champion parade in the catalogues.

One lovely thing about the February landscape is that I can look out and not see one solitary Japanese beetle anywhere on all our acres. And last summer the air was black with them. We did all the usual things to control them, and if we ever sat down to relax, a million more would begin champing their jaws on whatever they missed before.

We felt very bitter, for the Jap beetle is a newcomer in our valley. I for one feel the Government should make a war on this burden of mankind, allocating taxes and using the Army. One less bomb might be dropped in the ocean.

Some of the houses in the valley are closed now while their people are in Florida. They look lonely with the shutters locked close and the State Police signs on the doors. Icicles hang from the eaves in long silver needles, and they glitter in the sun with delicate splendor. Around the unshoveled walks the small prints of stay-at-home rabbits and winter birds make fascinating patterns. The evergreen plantings stand heavy with snow, lovely and pure and shining.

It is a fine thing to follow the warmth to the South, I always think, and I can imagine the bright skies and dazzling water and I should love to walk the long beaches and gather sprays of coral and mysterious fragile shells.

The trouble is, I love it right here, and having only one life and one self I can never quite resolve to shut up the little white house in the meadow and leave the cockers and Maeve and the cats while I investigate the delights of summer-in-winter. I do mean to go someday, but maybe not right now while the woodshed is filled with such nice old apple wood and the lighted windows at night make such a lovely glow on the drifts outside. Then too there are all those frozen vegetables and fruits in the freezer, no use letting them sit around until summer when the garden grows green again.

Also we have time now to play some of the records we like best, the symphonies and the folk songs and the concertos. Being snowed in has some advantages, we are not likely to be interrupted just at the climax of the Beethoven *Seventh*.

I am always surprised when city friends ask us, "What in the world do you do in the winter? Isn't it awfully lonesome?"

Well, nobody can be lonesome in the country. Or at least there is no reason to be. Living involves enough activity to keep the days flying, whether you walk to the woods for branches of bright evergreens for the house, or run out to gather fresh eggs or put new suet out for the hosts of birds, or shovel a path to the kennels. In the evening there are books, and there is music, records, or radio. Time to pop fluffy kernels of corn, roast apples, and if you feel like visiting with faraway friends you can write leisurely letters instead of those frantic postcards that go out in summer.

When the ice on the pond is black-green and smooth, all the skaters are out. The swift, accomplished ones glide in elegant designs over the surface, their skates ring sharply. Near the edges small fry tumble about in red and blue bunny suits. A bonfire leaps merrily in the cold air.

Somehow it pleases me more than a bathing beauty scene!

On cold dark Sunday afternoons, when the wind howls in the bare branches outside the windows and a wild and whirling scud of clouds marks the sky, we light the fire and turn on the radio.

I have no patience with people who say they do not like radio. It is like saying they do not like books just because they do not care for mystery stories. I myself do not like singing commercials nor soap operas nor the lavish giving of prizes to women who can name the President of the United States after three hints. But I forget all this when I can hear the Philharmonic and have a full hour of glorious music sweeping right into my small house. How fortunate we are, to stay comfortably at home and toast our toes and drink hot tea and at the same time hear the warm golden horns and the deep melancholy viols and the singing violins!

I shall never be too much accustomed to this wonder. Every time I feel a fresh delight.

Music is necessary to life. I like to think back to the time when wandering minstrels came to the great dark halls of the old castles and sang to their lutes. Or, before that, when the Greek chorus chanted under the brave Athenian skies. And even when some people got the idea that music must be a sin because it gave so much joy, I know there were small songs sung by women as they rocked their babies in the old wooden cradles. I doubt whether any power on earth could keep folks from singing.

For in some wondrous way music eases the heart, re-

freshes the spirit, lifts the imagination. And it can fit any
mood, grave or gay. Just why the arrangements of sound
striking the ear can do all this is a mystery I have never
made plain to myself. Why are some chords, for instance,
as sad as tears? And some so light and gay they are like
spring flowers?

However, so it is.

I can remember when I was a little girl and the first
phonograph came to our town. It had a purple morning-
glory horn and small round discs that scratched out thin
reedy tunes.

It belonged to the family of one of the boys in my crowd,
and the minute it was set up in the parlor on the table I
decided this special boy was the nicest one I ever knew.
I would go to his house with him any day so we could
play those tunes. My devotion lasted until I met a new
boy who could play the piano by ear!

Later, when radio came in and KDKA began its his-
toric course, I listened faithfully even when all that ever
came over was *tweet, tweet, bang, bong*. We never heard
more than a few notes of each number but we thought
they were superb, and indeed they were the sunrise of
a world of sound.

Reading aloud is another kind of music that my ear likes.
On winter evenings, it is fine to read Edna St. Vincent
Millay or Shakespeare or Keats, or just to pick a book at
random and find some old favorite sonnet. The only kind
of poetry that seems authentic to me is that which sounds
like music when it is properly read. And the sound should

make its shape. By this I mean that printing the lines huggermugger in patterns on the page, or using no capitals, or running words together has little to do with the real poem. Also I do not like confused images that a reader with a reasonable amount of intelligence cannot follow. Great poetry is understandable.

It is usually the people who have nothing much to say that try to say it in such strange manner that it seems important. But to feel truth deeply and convey it truly— there is the great art.

> "There is a wind where the rose was,
> Cold rain where sweet grass was,
> And stars like sheep
> Stream o'er the steep
> Grey sky where the lark was."

How simple de la Mare sounds, and how the mood is evoked! Or Yeats:

> "We sat grown quiet at the name of love;
> We saw the last embers of daylight die,
> And in the trembling blue-green of the sky
> A moon, worn as if it had been a shell
> Washed by time's waters as they rose and fell
> About the stars and broke in days and years."

I once, long ago, heard Yeats read his poetry, and my volume is marked with the lines he chose. I wandered about in a dream for days, and since I was in school this did my lessons no good. But it was an experience I would cherish always, and now when I reach on the shelf and pull out the book, the magic evening comes back to me, the golden reading of the shimmering poetry.

I dare say Mr. Yeats would have been amused if he had known the girl in the front row with large eyes and feverish bright cheeks was being dedicated to poetry at that minute—and in time would name a red Irish setter girl for his great Queen Maeve!

When the day is done, the music over, and the books put away, the cockers settle by the hearth and Esmé speaks a few words in Siamese with regard to a bedtime snack of cream. Honey is willing to consider a snack too.

Visitors are beginning to ask me now how old Honey is, but Honey and I do not answer. I know we have been together a long while as calendar time goes, for we have done many things together, started up a mort of rabbits, polished up a lot of turkey and chicken scraps.

And to a casual eye, I know Honey looks like an old lady limping along slowly beside me. But not to me. To me she is as young and beautiful as she ever was, and I suspect that love always has this quality. To love someone is to see them forever young, forever fair. The accident of passing time has nothing to do with the spirit.

Honey now sleeps on the rosewood sofa in my bedroom, and if I wake up in the night I can look over and see her golden paws folded under her chin, one ear trailing over the edge of the sofa. Little Sister skips to the bed and curls like a bunny. The others who are taking their turn in the house distribute themselves in chairs and on the davenport in the living room. There is always a low light burning, so if any human gets up and wanders around the house no cocker will get stepped on.

Honey Lies by the Franklin Stove

We learned this the hard way when I got up one night for some aspirin and fell over a small sleeper in the doorway. The din was terrific, and I was in bed with a very black eye for two days. The cocker, however, was undamaged except in sensibilities.

Letter writing is another good part of snowbound days. There are special friends and relatives that I like to visit lavishly with, and this takes time. I have neighbors in many places all over the world that I can write to and hear from in these days. For instance, there is a woman in

Alaska whose husband is a trapper. They live in a kind of scow tied offshore, and she keeps house in a small cabin on the scow. She has an old rotting rowboat on the shore in which she has, in season, her garden. I have never seen this woman, but we are friends because we correspond about our gardens, mine in New England behind a white picket fence and hers in that old rowboat in Alaska. We also trade recipes, although I cook on an electric range and she cooks on a galley stove. There is another woman in Rhodesia; and one in Caracas, Venezuela; and one in Bristol, England. We have so much to say to one another about our houses, our dogs or cats, our gardens!

Pictures of the children can be exchanged or snaps of the countryside. All last fall I kept on my desk a colored picture of a garden in New Brunswick, Canada, which another woman had made herself. There was a wide sweep of color, and the planting was beside deep clear water; it was beautiful, and I felt as if I could walk there any minute and be at home. When I think how much in common women have all over the world, I entertain no thoughts of any more war, for I know if I could have letters from them, the women in Russia would like just the same things I like and want the same things for the world that we want in this country.

We might seem isolated at the end of our narrow country road, but we are not at all. Our neighbors are legion. Two of our very best neighbors belong to that group that seldom is thought of in connection with home things. But we know better, for Dallas and Smiley Burnette, who live in North Hollywood, are very dear neighbors. Smiley is a movie actor in Westerns, and I have a picture of their four children, their pool, and their dogs. And when Smiley was coming East on a personal appearance tour, he asked his agent to route him in New England as near Stillmeadow as possible.

And what could be more wonderful than a ballad about our forty acres in the New England valley written by this singer from the hills of Hollywood? And there it was, a song:

### ESPECIALLY STILLMEADOW

Closing my eyes, I will daydream awhile
Let my thoughts take me far, far away
Back to Stillmeadow with its babbling brooks,
That farm up Connecticut way.

Tigger and Esmé asleep in the sun,
Hildegarde's like a rug on the floor,
Honey and Melody wait on the stoop
For someone to open the door.

Guests are arriving, there's more by and by,
Jill's bustling round with chickens to fry,
Perfume from the kitchen says fresh cherry pie
On the farm up Connecticut way.

All are gone home, and the moon's ridin' high,
Then Honey and you climb the hill;
Fragrance of apples is heavy and sweet,
The orchard is lovely and still.

The lights from the house help the moon light the yard,
In the night there's a late-flying bird,
Breathe deep the air from the cool evening breeze
And know why a prayer will be heard.

Poems are written and songs will be sung,
But no fitting description will find any tongue,
The thrill from the hill when the evening is young
From a farm up Connecticut way!

Now what could make a lovelier valentine, or better express that friendship which all home folks share, no matter where they are?

## CHAPTER TWELVE

March is exciting. Wild wind winnowing the fields of winter and the brown, good, wet earth showing, and the washed blue of the sky, and the brook running mad by the Phillips' barn. There is the smell of spring in the air, and the feeling of spring in the heart. In my childhood, the carpets were out on the line by now, beaten with big wire whisks, and the front porches were scrubbed and freshly painted gray or mustard. The most vigorous housewives emptied every room and threw most things out-of-doors—pillows, curtains, sofa covers. I know what it was: they were done with winter, they wanted to let spring into the very cracks of the furniture.

Blankets blossomed on every line; mattresses came out the first dry day, too, and the intricate washing of coil bedsprings enlisted little girls like me who wanted to ride their bicycles wildly all over town. Spring cleaning went on into April, but came a day at last when the smallest spoon shone and the smell of furniture polish penetrated every carved drawer pull.

The whole town had the cleanest, crispest look, with every yard raked, every walk spotless, and in the gardens the clean shoots of tulips pushing up. Then Mamma always felt like having a party, and fried spring chicken was just right, with plenty of creamy gravy with crispy bits left in from the frying, whipped potatoes with parsley topping, peas with mint, lime salad ring, and a simple little dessert like Lady Baltimore cake.

At Stillmeadow, we no longer go in for a month-long cleaning. We clean when the spirit moves, which with me usually means a fit of depression. Nothing like a bout with bureau drawers to make one's world seem better, for there is a simple and direct satisfaction in a tangible task well done. And when the house is clean and ordered, there is new serenity in it. Besides, say what you will, if you are working hard, you don't have energy left over for brooding.

I heard a woman lecturer a short time ago saying American women were enslaved by household drudgery. Selling their souls, she said, when they should be pursuing the higher things in life. This was the time I lost my temper, which happens about once in six months. She went on to say young married women spent too much time on their children and their houses and fixing up for their husbands. At that moment, I could see the walls of the room turning a slow red.

For it seemed to me her attitude was medieval—born in the era when only the low peasant classes did anything with their hands. The noble folk embroidered or chased deer. And she thought she was ultra-ultra modern! To make a home beautiful, to create a good family life, seems to me a job as important and dignified as any, and there is no reason why pushing a vacuum cleaner is incompatible with thinking about Plato or Aristotle or Parker's *Aesthetics*. The truth is, I thought, saying nothing while she monologued on, that any job is according to the person performing it. My mother, for instance, was never a career woman; she had no college degree, she was a housewife. But her heart was wise, her intelligence was keen, and the memory of her is still a shining thing for many people that I know about. And if this lecturer with her shaggy fierce look had met Mother and they had conversed, the odds would have been entirely Mother's. Inside of a short while, Mother would have found out what was really wrong and, without seeming to, have suggested something to ease the bitterness that sharpened the attack on the enslaved American wives.

I love to drive through our valley at dusk and see the white houses and the people coming home for supper. And the violet light on the crocus buds by the front door. I like to see the bicycles leaning on the steps and the scooters drawn up with relaxed wheels. It gives me a good feeling.

One of the nicest things ever said to me came in the mail today from an eighty-five-year-old lady far away. It is something special, like a gift, and it made the whole new spring world lovelier. She said, "Your imagination makes life wear wings." Suddenly I realized that life can always wear wings, if we will have it so. It was a secret for living that she had discovered and expressed. Imagination isn't always dodging reality, either, but it's things like doing dishes and playing Vienna waltzes and feeling, instead of like an enslaved drudge, like a "fortunate breather of the air" who can hear the swish of satin and the soft purr of velvet and the light tap of enchanted slippers from the past.

Imagination can invest any dull task with a glow. Even peeling potatoes, which is the worst job in the world to me, can acquire interest. I always face a large pan of million-eyed potatoes with a very sour look, and then I reach for the knife and decide to think about something very special and nice or exciting until the last peel spirals into the sink strainer.

It is fun for the mind to make a journey beginning with potatoes. I may start—Ireland: Digging potatoes in the green land of Eire. Little thatched cottages, peat bogs, jaunting cars. Irish smugglers off a dark coast on windy nights long ago (here I dive easily into the past). Then Irish faery folk come to mind—Deidre and Cuchulainn and the shadowy horses and the little silver trout that turned in the pan and spoke. The changeling, and the child the faeries stole away—these are fine tales. I can say Yeats' words: "For he comes, the human child, To the waters and the wild, With a faery, hand in hand, From a world more full of weeping than he can understand."

How often for most of us the world is more full of weeping than we can understand!

But by now I am come back from the past and the land between the worlds, for the pan is filled with peeled potatoes and the chore is over. Maybe as I carry the peelings out for the hens, I finish with a bit of Yeats I especially like.

> "Shy one, shy one,
> Shy one of my heart,
> She moves in the firelight
> Pensively apart.
>
> "She carries in the dishes
> And lays them in a row.
> To an isle in the water
> With her I would go."

Departing winter brings a new crop of stones and boulders from the bottom of Connecticut. No matter how often we clear the garden, there is a new crop by spring, mysteriously rising, and yet who ever has seen the rising of a stone? One day there it is, where yesterday there was good dirt.

It reminds me of a friend of ours who moved here and began feverishly to move rocks from a prospective vegetable patch. An old farmer walked down the road and looked on awhile, puffing at his old pipe. Finally he said, "We don't move the rocks in Connecticut, we plant around them."

This would be a fine rule to observe with human obstacles sometimes! Now and then I see someone working hopelessly at a really tough proposition, and I feel like saying, "Just plant around it."

Actually I like the stones. The old gray stone fences are beautiful any time of year, and nice places for squirrels and chipmunks. Bittersweet can find a purchase in them, and birds light comfortably on the tipmost stone. And they mark the ways of earlier folk in our valley, for every rock was put in place by some clearer of the land. A stone fence is a quiet testimonial to the will of man to make the land fruitful.

Outcropping on the hills, the great ledges stir the heart with a sense of permanence in the universe. The handwriting of time lies upon them in the deep glacial scratches, this was the way the great ice moved. Now the rosy delicate lichens and velvety mosses inscribe a transient signature.

When the ledges begin to feel warm, I know winter is gone. Life is beginning again, as new and wonderful as if this were the first time the ice and snow had gone on. The water of the pond will dissolve the last fretwork of ice along the bank and be free again to drink the sun and moon.

We scarcely notice the buds on the lilacs and maples in winter although they are set in autumn, but suddenly on a warm day we see buds everywhere, polished and compact with life. The grass, which is deader than anything I know of, all at once has a green look to it, as if it had all been brushed with a paint brush dipped in spring.

I notice a change in the people too. Villagers speak in livelier tones, the women seem gay as they come into the grocery store. The children bounce in and out, small boys jiggle their marbles in muddy hands. Two little girls in red and blue jackets sit on the steps of the post office playing jacks.

In the market, fresh crisp little kittens dash around and Louie's dachshund emerges to the stoop. Joe slices the great wheel of cheddar and sings *Easter Parade* in his beautiful clear young voice. As I nibble a crumb of cheese, I wonder dreamily why any man so beautiful as Joe is not on the screen, but I am very glad he is not but is right in Southbury. When he and Louie put away their uniforms and settled right down in the home place, we were all delighted.

I do think a lamb chop tastes better if it has been wrapped with a smile. I am easily discouraged by salespeople who are severe or irritable. I always decide I will just go home without whatever I planned to buy. But if I am warmly greeted, I can always think of a good deal of shopping that I may as well do now.

Often in the city, I hear the women customers abusing the salesgirls. Women around a bargain counter make me feel ashamed of myself for being a woman. I do hope being rude to people who serve you is not typically American. It is certainly prevalent. If there is a line at a counter in a department store, some woman always gets ahead of the rest and has her parcel five minutes earlier, but what an expensive five minutes that is. Is it really worth being hateful and aggressive and vindictive to be the head of the line? I doubt it. What does she do with that five minutes?

It must be pretty valuable to have sacrificed being a lady for it.

*Esmé Sleeps in the Window*

I think it is better to be like my mother was, for after she died every clerk in the whole town who had ever sold her a paper of pins was as sincerely grieved as if a personal friend had gone, as indeed she had. Years later, one said to me, "I was always glad to see your mother come in the store, I still miss seeing her walk in with her sweet smile."

This is a lovely memorial for a person to have, I think. The only kind of memorial that is really worth having.

If one could be sure that, all through life, everyone was always glad to see one—this is pleasant to contemplate as a successful career.

The day the storm windows come off is a day of rejoicing to me. It is just as if the house didn't need to wear spectacles any longer. There is a brief period before the screens must go on, and when the windows are open the outdoors comes right in. So, also, does Esmé. When she can leap in and out without bothering to scream at the doors, she is happy, and we are more quiet. Maeve cannot quite get all of her large red self in, but she can hang half of her on the sill and reach muddy paws in and look appealing. Someone has to rush to open the door before her paws ruin the white woodwork and the wallpaper.

For an old house, the storm windows are a real necessity. Fragile old panes and narrow frames keep out little cold. Pale drifts of snow used to filter in too and lie on the sills. Now we are dry and warm all winter, but oh how wonderful to fling up the windows and let the March wind in!

Window washing is not my favorite sport, but if I have to wash windows I would rather wash them for spring than wash them double—inside and outside, sash and storm sash too!

Father used to have quite a time with the storm windows in our house when I was growing up. The house had seventy-two windows, and a heavy plate-glass storm window for every one. Father never procrastinated about things, he always wanted to get done with anything at once. So he began to get restless early in September. "I better get the storm windows on," he would say.

Mamma would protest. We would suffocate with the heat. But the next thing we knew, Father would be lugging the big ladder from the garage and skipping up.

The house would be battened down for winter, and then we always had a very hot spell. It would be eighty inside, and Mamma would be cross. And then around the end of February, Father would get that look in his blue eyes. "May as well take off the storm windows," he would decide during the February thaw. "Spring will be here any minute!"

Mamma would protest again. But out came the ladder and off came the storm sash, and of course we would get some bad blizzards thereafter. Father might be annoyed with the weather, but he himself had, as usual, done the right thing. It wasn't his fault it snowed.

He always had trouble getting ahead of things. When he planted a garden, he put the seeds in so early they froze. Now and then he would dig up a few just to see if they were minding their business. Nature was too slow for him. He always had the auto ready for winter too soon so the radiator kept boiling over because it was just too warm for all that alcohol.

He rarely condoned tire chains, on the theory that he could drive well enough on ice without them. When he did have them on, if he came to a single good spot on the road he hopped out and took the chains off, and we skidded the rest of the way.

Father also always got up shortly after dawn, on the theory that "If you don't get started you'll never accomplish anything."

Maybe the present generation is weaker than his, for I could never approximate his rapid pace through time and I know of none of my friends who can either. When I have to get up at five to catch a train or for some imperative reason, I appreciate how much extra time there can be in a day.

And the coming of day is so mysterious. The blackness seems suddenly to be tenuous, not thick and deep. It is just as dark and yet the dark has no body to it, somehow. Then along the horizon a faint pale band of pure color begins to glow, first the color of the breast of a gull, then a wash of rosy pearl, and finally a deep apricot with lacings of fire.

By now the rest of the universe gives itself to light, and the hills are distinct in the dove-colored day. The hollows keep small cups of night for a little, and then the whole sky and earth all at once flash into the splendor of the new sun.

I suppose if we really went in for daylight saving the whole way, we would have the whole country begin the morning at daybreak, and end the day at dusk. The only trouble would be that we would lose a lot of evening, and evening can be very pleasant.

There are so many nice things to do when the work of the day is tucked away behind one. Or, if one works then, there is a sense of leisure about the work, for one does not have to watch to see when to jump up and start getting a meal.

I love to read in bed. There is a feeling of luxury about tucking in comfortably with a new book, which opens some fresh world, with a cocker or two snugged down at my feet and a plate of cheese and crackers and a glass of milk on the table.

For music there is the sound of the peepers and the faint crackle of the last log in the fireplace in the family room.

The New England countryside is as clean as a silver whistle now, swept by wild winds, washed by melting snowdrifts, garnished by new buds. This is the season of hope, the stirring of fresh life, this is the year really new.

For me, the new world begins in beauty on a March morning when I look out the window and see the flying scud of white clouds against a gentian sky. How wonderful it would be if I could paint the wind on such a morning! Or catch the symphony of sound in music.

The cockers get a kind of spring dementia. They race around in frantic circles, their ears standing out like sails. Their tails do stay on, but nobody knows why. Maeve looks redder than ever and is in a hunting mood. She and George's dog, Shep, go up the hill after woodchucks. Shep is a sensible fellow and Maeve is such a temperamental setter that they make an odd pair. Maeve loves to sneak up behind Shep and grab his tail and swing back on it, and when the big shepherd turns about, she whisks away, laughing heartily. He evens the score by not allowing her to ride on his truck with him when he goes with George to the fields. She has to run beside it.

An Irish setter running is a poem. A cocker is a lyric when he runs, but the long, level flight of a setter is an ode.

March meals are hearty at our house. When one exercises outdoors half the day, dinner must "stick to the ribs," as Mamma used to say. *Sauerbraten* does just that, and is good for supper when the neighbors drop in.

Our village is growing. We now have a radio shop and a drugstore, besides the grocery store, garage, and post office. It is utterly strange to drive to the triangle where the roads meet and step into a modern drugstore, right out here in our valley. The radio shop hadn't been open a day before we were there with two radios, and it was very pleasant to get first aid for the sound waves within a couple of miles from the house.

But it is true that I do not like change, and I kept saying I liked the old days better, even while I was getting tooth paste and soap from the nice new druggist. I can foresee the day when we shall not really be countryfolk any more, but a kind of extended suburbanites.

However, Jill says bitterly, we don't get any express service any more, so progress isn't quite swamping us. They took that away this season. When express comes, it arrives ten miles on one side or ten miles on the other, according to the whim of the express company, apparently, or it may turn up in Newtown. Freight all goes there.

I am glad we got the house furnished before the express

withdrew, because I really do not see how anybody could possibly get a piano delivered any more in our parts. It is a queer and mysterious fact that as civilization—or the outward evidences of it—spreads farther and farther into the hinterlands, at the same time it also retreats. I suppose this is another thing that is peculiarly American.

The snowdrops are out around the twenty-second. The lovely pearl-white bells seem too delicate to bear the brunt of that March wind, but they do. The first clump that opens is a cause for special celebration. The scilla is fragile, too, and so is the first pale amethyst crocus. Bloodroot and dog-tooth violets—all the flowers of spring seem too frail to last out the end of the cold. And they are all the more exquisite because they seem so alone in the world.

When the peepers begin to cry in the night, I like to lie awake just to listen to the sweet, thin crying. No music can compare with it, for it is the voice of new life beginning, or a new season coming; it is the final period to the silent sentences of winter.

The swamp still looks dark and wintry in the cold light of the moon, but in the swamp all the little folk are stirring, and the brave song makes the heart glad.

Surely, I think, there is no grief so deep that might not be eased by the sound of the singing in spring, no joy so perfect that might not seem even better.

Without the long winter, would we love the spring so much? I will leave that to the philosophers to answer. For myself, I can just go up to the old orchard on the top of the hill, with Honey puffing beside me, and let the great sweep of the wind blow away everything tired and old and sad and bring the sweet thunder in the blood of spring!